ORIGAMI
IKEBANA

ORIGAMI
IKEBANA

CREATE LIFELIKE PAPER FLOWER ARRANGEMENTS

Benjamin John Coleman

TUTTLE Publishing

Tokyo | Rutland, Vermont | Singapore

Published by Tuttle Publishing, an imprint of
Periplus Editions (HK) Ltd.

www.tuttlepublishing.com

Library of Congress Cataloging data in
process

ISBN: 978-4-8053-1242-1

DISTRIBUTED BY
North America, Latin America & Europe
Tuttle Publishing
364 Innovation Drive
North Clarendon, VT 05759-9436 U.S.A.
Tel: (802) 773-8930
Fax: (802) 773-6993
info@tuttlepublishing.com
www.tuttlepublishing.com

Japan
Tuttle Publishing
Yaekari Building, 3rd Floor
5-4-12 Osaki
Shinagawa-ku
Tokyo 141 0032
Tel: (81) 3 5437-0171
Fax: (81) 3 5437-0755
sales@tuttle.co.jp
www.tuttle.co.jp

Asia Pacific
Berkeley Books Pte. Ltd.
61 Tai Seng Avenue #02-12
Singapore 534167
Tel: (65) 6280-1330
Fax: (65) 6280-6290
inquiries@periplus.com.sg
www.periplus.com

First edition
18 17 16 15 14   5 4 3 2 1   1402EP

Printed in Hong Kong

This book is dedicated to Caroline and Frank Stewart who volunteered to teach my classmates and me origami at an afterschool program at Nathan Bishop Middle School in Providence, Rhode Island during the spring of 1977. Had they not given their time, this book might not exist.

THE TUTTLE STORY

"Books to Span the East and West"

Many people are surprised to learn that the world's largest publisher of books on Asia had its humble beginnings in the tiny American state of Vermont. The company's founder, Charles E. Tuttle, belonged to a New England family steeped in publishing.

Tuttle's father was a noted antiquarian dealer in Rutland, Vermont. Young Charles honed his knowledge of the trade working in the family bookstore, and later in the rare books section of Columbia University Library. His passion for beautiful books—old and new—never wavered throughout his long career as a bookseller and publisher.

After graduating from Harvard, Tuttle enlisted in the military and in 1945 was sent to Tokyo to work on General Douglas MacArthur's staff. He was tasked with helping to revive the Japanese publishing industry, which had been utterly devastated by the war. After his tour of duty was completed, he left the military, married a talented and beautiful singer, Reiko Chiba, and in 1948 began several successful business ventures.

To his astonishment, Tuttle discovered that postwar Tokyo was actually a book-lover's paradise. He befriended dealers in the Kanda district and began supplying rare Japanese editions to American libraries. He also imported American books to sell to the thousands of GIs stationed in Japan. By 1949, Tuttle's business was thriving, and he opened Tokyo's very first English-language bookstore in the Takashimaya Department Store in Ginza, to great success. Two years later, he began publishing books to fulfill the growing interest of foreigners in all things Asian.

Though a westerner, Tuttle was hugely instrumental in bringing a knowledge of Japan and Asia to a world hungry for information about the East. By the time of his death in 1993, he had published over 6,000 books on Asian culture, history and art—a legacy honored by Emperor Hirohito in 1983 with the "Order of the Sacred Treasure," the highest honor Japan can bestow upon a non-Japanese.

The Tuttle company today maintains an active backlist of some 1,500 titles, many of which have been continuously in print since the 1950s and 1960s—a great testament to Charles Tuttle's skill as a publisher. More than 60 years after its founding, Tuttle Publishing is more active today than at any time in its history, still inspired by Charles Tuttle's core mission—to publish fine books to span the East and West and provide a greater understanding of each.

Contents

THE WORLD OF PLANTS

Our planet is bursting with life. Wherever you look, if you take the time to look, you will find things growing. There are few places on earth where life does not exist, at least life that we're capable of comprehending. And within this bounty of species of living things, perhaps the largest group of individual life forms is plants. From simple blades of grass to highly complex fruit-producing trees, plants dominate the earth.

That we are dependent upon plants is obvious. Our clothing is made from plants. We consume them at every meal. We modify and mass produce them. We are so heavily dependent upon them that even slight changes in our ability to grow plants will result in massive loss of human life. We have harnessed power that only plants possess to gain dominion over our planet.

At the same time we have a unique, unseen and intimate relationship with plants. This relationship is centered on flowers. To us, flowers are beautiful and powerful things. Their delicate, complex beauty seems temporary, however when human interaction and emotion is added, a simple flower may be remembered by two people for a lifetime. One flower, picked by one person, and in a fleeting moment, given to another person, is often a catalyst for the cycle that results in new generations of people. It is easy to imagine that among people, this flower-powered catalyst existed long before language did!

A quick study of a flower's reproductive cycle will reveal a fundamental truth. That millennia ago flowers gave birth to us. I believe that this is why flowers maintain so much power over us. I believe this connection hasn't been forgotten and is still embedded within us.

A NEW WAY OF FLOWER ARRANGING

Honestly, I'm not really interested in conventional flower arrangements; at least the ones I've been exposed to. Most arrangements seem to be based on overabundance rather than scarcity. They emphasize symmetry rather than irregularity. Control as opposed to wilderness. Why would a symmetrical arrangement of an overabundant plant be appealing to anyone except the person who arranged it? I had not considered that there might be another way to display flowers.

About three years ago a friend looked at one of my sculptures and said, "Ikebana!" I said, "Ike-what?" To which he responded, "Japanese flower arranging." When looked up the term on the Web, my screen filled with images, and my jaw dropped. For the first time I was seeing plants, not just flowers, treated with the respect I believe they deserve. These arrangements seemed to honor life in a way I do not pretend to understand.

I don't know how to explain my feelings surrounding ikebana arrangements. All I can tell you is that I have felt this way before. In my younger days, exploring life around me, I occasionally stumbled upon scenes of amazing, indescribable beauty. Perhaps I'd be lying on my stomach, looking at a moss covered rock. First I'd notice the texture of the rock, then the moss, then the interactions between colors and textures. Then I'd notice that a small flower had taken root in an adjacent crevice. And then a feeling would come from deep within. The feeling was a mixture of satisfaction, happiness and calm—a serenity mixed with excitement. Some of the ikebana pictures I saw that first day evoked this feeling in me.

Since that time I have dreamed of developing techniques that would allow me to mimic ikebana-style arrangements. I cannot how far I've progressed. However, this book is testament to what I've accomplished. With tools; paper, paint and glue, one can never duplicate the complex beauty of even a single blade of grass, much less a flower's petal. But perhaps we can capture some of the essence of ikebana.

In this book I've tried to honor plants like never before. By combining ikebana, origami, and makigami techniques, I seek to create sculptures that shed new light on the human-plant relationship. Instead of planters, I will show you how to build arrangements on stone-like structures made from paper. This will allow us to explore textures without the expense of buying ceramics made specifically for ikebana arrangements. I will teach you how to make these arrangements, and together we will explore a world of ikebana-inspired origami flower arrangements the likes of which have never been seen before.

How to Use This Book

This book was written for both experienced and inexperienced folders. The diagrams you'll find in this book are different; they employ a new technique called *glow-fold* which is explained on the opposite page. It is unlikely that you'll read through this book from front to back. It is more likely that you'll use this book like a reference tool, skipping back and forth to different sections as you need them. I recommend keeping at least two bookmarks handy.

Origami paper is expensive. The best place to begin in this book is in the section, "Cutting Paper for Origami Ikebana" (page 16). As a general rule, when learning, or when practicing, you should use inexpensive squares you have cut yourself.

Rules for Faster Origami Learning

MAKE PRACTICE PAPER BEFORE YOU BEGIN
Jump ahead to page 16 and make some practice squares. This will allow you to make your mistakes on inexpensive practice squares instead of expensive origami paper.

THE EFFECTS OF AN INCORRECTLY MADE FOLD INCREASE AS THE MODEL PROGRESSES
I have seen students struggle because they refuse to throw away the square they started with. They continue using the same piece of paper despite making one incorrect fold. They proceed, successfully completing a few more folds, and then make another incorrect fold. What most folders don't realize is that an incorrect fold at the beginning compounds exponentially as we progress through a folding pattern. By the time the folder nears the end, the incorrect fold has contaminated almost every plane of their model. Something inside us tells us not to waste paper, however "wasting paper" when exploring a new folding pattern will end up saving both paper and time in the long run. Just don't forget to recycle those discarded attempts.

REVIEW THE INSTRUCTIONS BEFORE FOLDING THE MODEL
Before you begin, look at each diagram and read each instruction. This allows your brain a little time to review the pattern before you attempt it. Even if you don't fully understand the diagrams and instructions, reviewing them in advance will give you an edge and save you time and paper.

WATCH THE VIDEO
If you have trouble making any of the base models in this book, take a look at the videos on the accompanying DVD.

EXPLORE THE ACCOMPANYING DVD
The DVD that comes with this book has several computer template files you may find helpful.

INTRODUCING *GLOW-FOLD* INSTRUCTIONS

Glow-fold is a new, patented diagramming method for conveying folding. It is particularly useful for origami instructions. *Glow-fold* works by highlighting the surface of the area which will move during the fold with an orange, semi-transparent glow. In the diagram immediately following, a narrow trace of orange semi-transparent glow will be visible along any open edges. This narrow trace is called *afterglow* and indicates where the glowing surface went. Afterglow appears only along edges were the initial glow would normally leak through; in other words, there won't be afterglow along the folded side of the area that just moved.

Glow-fold dramatically decreases the time it takes to learn a new folding pattern. Instead of trial and error style experimentation, glow-fold allows the folder to navigate diagrams with confidence. It turns the process of completing a new model from a frustrating puzzle into a coherent step-by-step progression. This diagramming system makes origami accessible to scores of people who thought they didn't have the patience to do origami.

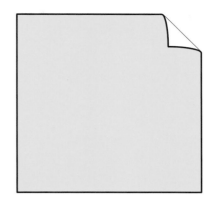

1 We begin with a square piece of paper. It is yellow on one side and white on the other. We start with the yellow side facing us.

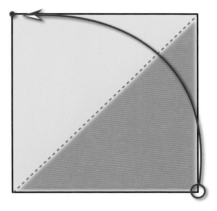

2 We're going to fold the square in half on a diagonal. Notice that there's a glow on top of the triangle formed by the bottom and right edges, and the diagonal (marked by a dashed green line) where the paper is to be folded.

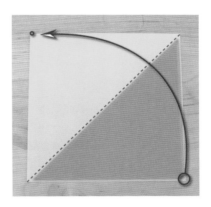

3 Imagine the overlay on top of the square in front of you. It would look like this, and you would fold the bottom right corner up to the top left corner.

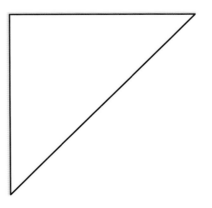

4 The next diagram would look like this. Notice that there is a narrow band of orange afterglow along the top and left edges. This afterglow represents light that would leak out along the open edges. There is no afterglow along the fold because light from the original glow would not leak out there.

SYMBOLS, TIPS, AND TOOLS

The Fold Symbol and the Proper Way to Fold

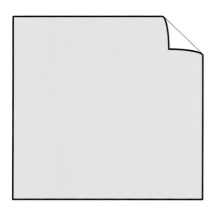

1 I'm using a square piece of paper which is yellow on one side and white on the other.

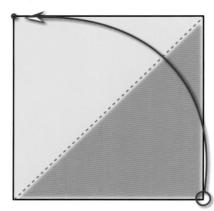

2 The arc with a circle on one end and an arrowhead pointing to a tiny circle on the other is called the *folding symbol*. In this instance it means you should fold the square in half diagonally.

3 To properly make this fold, begin by lifting the bottom right corner and lining it up with the upper right corner. I am curling and not folding the paper.

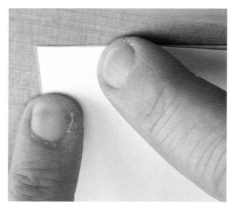

4 Very carefully align the corners so that they perfectly match (for illustrative purposes, my corners are slightly out of alignment in this photo).

5 Hold the corner down firmly with your left index finger while you apply pressure to the curl with the fingers on your right hand.

6 Commit the fold with your index finger.

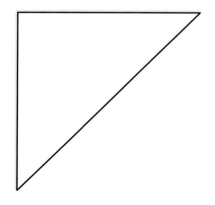

7 Your model should look like this.

The Flip Symbol

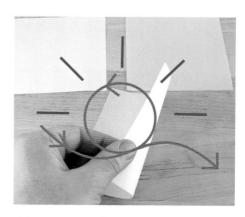

When you see the flip symbol you should turn your paper over.

Fold and then Unfold Symbol

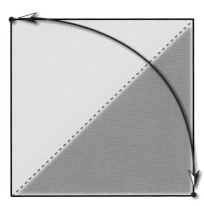 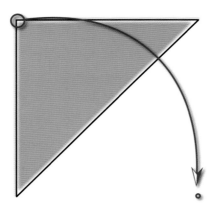 

1 This is the fold and unfold symbol. When you see this symbol you should perform all the steps for the fold symbol just as you did on the top of the opposite page.

2 Now unfold the fold you made.

3 Your square should look like this. Notice that the fold you just made is represented by a narrow line. Normally there won't be afterglow associated with the fold and then unfold symbol, although I did add afterglow to this diagram to show you where the surface in step 2 went.

The Fold on Both Sides Symbol

 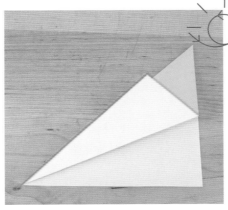 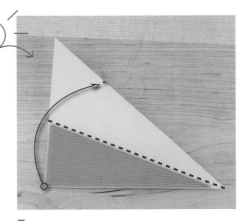

1 When you see this symbol, begin by performing the fold indicated on the side facing you.

2 Next, flip your model.

3 Perform the mirror image of the fold you made in step 1 on the other side of your model.

 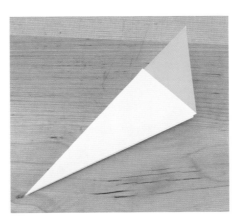

4 Your model would look like this. Next, flip it.

5 Now you have performed the same fold on both sides of your model.

SYMBOLS, TIPS, AND TOOLS

How to Make a Crush-Fold

We make crush-folds in almost every leaf we create. We also use the crush-fold in step 19 of the Basic Flower Form (page 44). Making a good crush fold is a challenge, but obsessing over it is a complete waste of time. None of the crush-folds described in this book will be visible in a completed sculpture.

1 A crush-fold is called for whenever there's a pocket created by another fold. Narrowing the stem of this leaf created two pockets. We're going to crush-fold the pocket on the right.

2 All you do is crush the pocket with a finger.

3 Notice that the pocket on the right has been flattened.

How to Make a Pinch-Fold

A pinch-fold is required whenever there isn't an easy way to make the fold. A pinch-fold, in this book, will always be made on an existing fold line. I also use the same symbol to denote pushing the paper (see the next section).

You will find a detailed explanation of the pinch-fold on page 43.

How to Make a Collapse and the Push Symbol

A collapse is a complex fold where your model folds into itself. The most familiar item you've seen collapse-fold is an umbrella. The fold is made up of pre-installed folds which set up the collapse. This fold will seem impossible at first, until suddenly your square collapses!

You will find a detailed explanation of a collapse on page 45.

How to Make a Book-Fold

We call it a book-fold because it's just like turning the pages of a book. This fold always involves a shape that has several layers. The layers are usually connected to an axis, just like a book's pages are connected to its binding. The layers can be rotated just like turning the pages of a book.

In this example, a flap is being book-folded from right to left. Notice that after the book-fold there will be three flaps on the left and only one on the right.

The Zoom Symbol

The zoom symbol means the scale in diagrams has changed between steps. As I fold a model it will get smaller, so I will increase the size of the diagrams so you can see them more clearly.

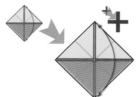

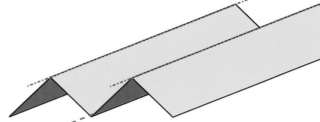

The zoom symbol indicates that the diagram scale has increased.

Mountain and Valley Folds

No origami book would be complete without an explanation of mountain and valley folds. The most important thing to remember is that almost every fold prescribed in this book is a valley fold. Valley folds are denoted by a green dashed line. On the rare occasion when there is a mountain fold, it will be denoted by a red dashed line.

Notice that the paper moves up on each side of a valley fold, and down on each side of a mountain fold.

Fold Quality

The quality of your folds is important. Most people think that a flap should be folded so that its edge lands as closely as possible to the reference line without going beyond it. In fact, most flaps created early in a model's folding pattern will become components of other flaps and points yet to be completed. Experienced folders have learned that it is important to leave a small gap, preferably about as wide as the thickness of two sheets of paper, between any edge and its reference line.

Always leave small gap between the edge of the surface being folded and the fold or edge it is being folded to.

If a fold needs to be reversed, always sharpen it. You can use a popsicle stick to sharpen folds on origami paper, but for painted paper you should use a wallpaper seam roller (shown in background).

Symbols Used in This Book

The fold symbol

The fold and then unfold symbol

The crush-fold symbol

The pinch-fold symbol

The collapse symbol

The flip symbol

The fold on both sides symbol

The book-fold symbol

SYMBOLS, TIPS, AND TOOLS

Tools and Supplies You Will Need

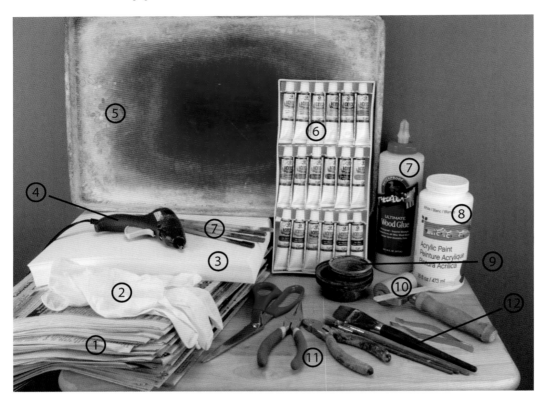

1. Newspaper
2. Latex gloves
3. Paper, either US 8 ½" x 11", or A4
4. Hot melt glue gun
5. Shallow pan, approximately 11 x 17 inches, or 28 x 43 centimeters
6. Assorted acrylic paints
7. Wood glue
8. A large quantity of white acrylic paint
9. Small, shallow cups for mixing paint
10. A wallpaper seam roller or a popsicle stick
11. Tools, including pliers, wire cutters, scissors and tweezers
12. Assorted brushes

    (not shown) Artist's medium bodied matte acrylic emulsion

The Web and Other Resources

There is a vast amount of origami-related information available in books and on the Web. I often add an origami hummingbird from one of my favorite books, *Advanced Origami* by Michael LaFosse (Tuttle, 2005). There are thousands of folding videos on YouTube.com and folding diagrams on websites like Scribd.com. Most importantly, there are two websites devoted to making botanical sculptures from paper, **www.Benagami.com** and **www.OrigamiBonsai.org**.

There are also numerous opportunities to sell your work online. Etsy, Artfire, and DaWanda are websites which offer inexpensive e-commerce for handmade goods. You'll need to figure out shipping costs, but other than that, these sites make selling your work really easy.

www.Benagami.com features my latest work and information about my studio.

www.OrigamiBonsai.org is a creative forum for people interested in making plants using origami and makigami techniques.

An origami hummingbird feeds at an origami flower.

How to Pack a Sculpture for Shipping

Whether you're selling your work or giving it away, you need to know how to ship your sculptures successfully. While origami ikebana arrangements look delicate, they're actually quite resilient when shipped because they have very little mass. This means the boxes they're shipped in can take a fair amount of abuse without damaging the sculpture inside. When packing your sculpture, be very careful when executing steps 1 and 6, described below. For full disclosure, I have to admit that I broke my sculpture's stamens in step 1. I would normally not put a sculpture inside a box as shown in step 1 without securing the flaps on one side first. Securing the flaps on one side ensures that the box won't collapse unexpectedly.

You should also consider double-boxing every sculpture you ship. In other words, pack the box as described below inside another, larger box. You should never put any additional loose items inside the inner box which contains the sculpture. Even something as small and light as an origami hummingbird can damage a sculpture during shipping when packed inside the inner box.

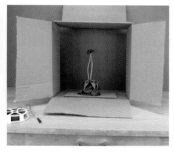

1 Find a box big enough to fit your sculpture with lots of room to spare. Cut a piece of cardboard that's a little bit smaller than one side of your box. Set your sculpture aside and open the flaps on both sides of the box.

2 Poke two holes through the piece of cardboard and the side of your box, at the front right corner and at the back left corner.

3 Mark the piece of cardboard and the box so you'll have a reference to align the holes you made in step 2.

4 Poke two more holes on the piece of cardboard, very close to the base of your arrangement. If you're shipping a very large sculpture you may want to poke four holes.

5 Use a twist tie to secure the sculpture to the piece of cardboard.

6 Secure the flaps on one side of the box by overlapping them. Align the piece of cardboard to the box using the mark you made. Thread a twist tie through the closest holes you made in the piece of cardboard and then through the corresponding holes you made in the side of the box, and then twist them to secure the piece of cardboard to the box. Close and secure the flaps on this side of the box with tape, and then open the flaps on the opposite side.

7 Repeat step 6 on this side of the piece of cardboard, and then close and secure these flaps with tape.

8 Write instructions for the recipient on the outside of the box as shown. They should open one side of the box and then cut the twist ties to release the piece of cardboard from the box. Make sure the twist ties are tight by twisting them a couple more times, and then secure their ends with small pieces of tape.

CUTTING PAPER FOR ORIGAMI IKEBANA

Leaves and flowers grow in every size imaginable. I was recently at a greenhouse which had some large palm trees. These trees had leaves that were over eight feet long. I have also seen trees, like some varieties of mesquite, that have leaflets which are almost microscopic. We must have a method for cutting squares in many sizes in order to mimic a variety of plant life.

When I first began making origami plant sculptures I used commercially produced squares of origami paper. Making lots of differently sized leaves was both expensive and wasteful. One day I ran out of origami paper. With an abundant supply of photocopy paper nearby, I wondered if I might be able to cut my own squares. What follows is a method that will make squares of just about any size.

How to Make Squares

This is a simple technique to make squares from inexpensive office paper. I prefer to use 20 lb. (75 gm/cm^2) paper with low or no rag (cotton) content. My latest batch is made entirely of recycled fibers and works well.

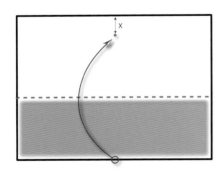

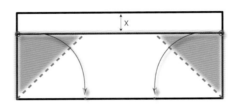

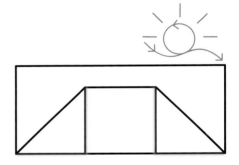

1 This first fold determines the size of your squares. The distance "X" represents the distance between the bottom and top edges of paper when the sheet is folded horizontally. If X=0 then you're folding the paper in half and you'll get the largest size squares. As X increases, your squares will decrease in size.

2 Fold the corners down and toward the center. Careful alignment will ensure you end up with good squares.

3 Your paper should look like this. Flip it left to right.

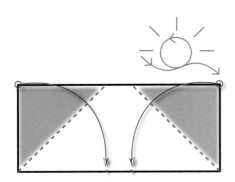

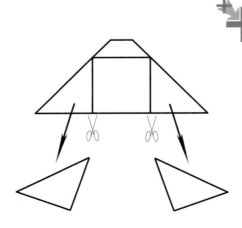

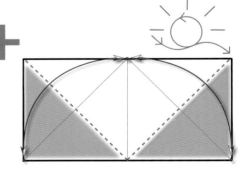

4 Fold the top corners down and toward the center just as you did in step 2, and then flip your model left to right.

5 Cut off and retain the two ends, and put the middle section into your paper recycling bin.

6 Completely unfold one of the triangles. Orient the rectangle so that both diagonal folds are valley folds and the center fold is a mountain fold. If you need two very large squares for leaves, cut the rectangle in half on the center fold line. If you'd like to make leaves ¼ the size or make flowers with these squares, fold and unfold each lower corner up to the center. Flip your rectangle.

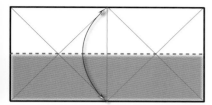

7 Fold and then unfold your rectangle in half horizontally.

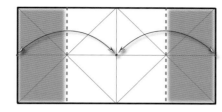

8 Fold and then unfold the left and right edges to the center.

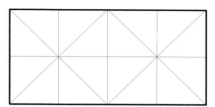

9 Your rectangle should look like this. You can cut it in half vertically to make two squares for flowers. Alternatively, if you'd like to make eight small leaves, you'll be cutting it horizontally and vertically *after you have painted it (see page 93)*.

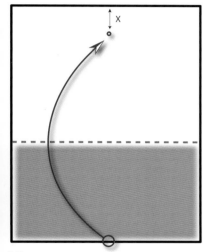

10 To make two larger squares, orient your paper vertically rather than horizontally in step 1.

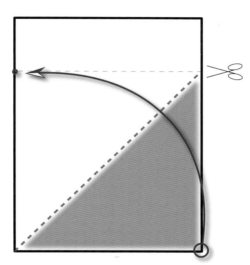

11 To make the largest possible square, fold diagonally and then cut the upper edge.

If you're making squares for leaves, wait until after you've painted the rectangle before cutting it.

CUTTING PAPER FOR ORIGAMI IKEBANA

How to Make Decagons for Five-Petal Flowers

You can print decagons on your printer using the templates provided on the DVD that came with this book. Start by printing the largest, from a file named 21-01 Decagon.png. When you print the file, make sure your computer doesn't automatically adjust the aspect ratio, which would stretch the outline. (Some programs do this to maximize the size of the printed image.) The aspect ratio must remain the same for the shape to be foldable.

You can also make your own decagons. My friend, Tanya Duffy, who lives in Australia, sent me this technique. Initially I was uncomfortable making some of the folds, but with a little practice, it works well. The advantage of making decagons in this manner is that all the initial folds you'd need to make in steps 1 and 2 of folding the Basic Flower Form (page 44) for an odd number of petals are made automatically as a by-product of creating the decagon.

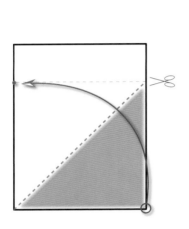

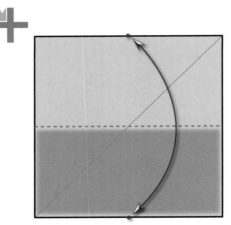

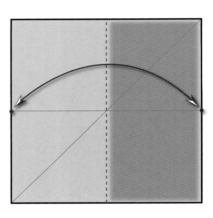

1 Begin by making two large square pieces of paper. We need to make one large square, and a second which is exactly ¼ its size to use as a measuring tool (see step 9). Set aside one of your squares. *To make smaller flowers, begin with smaller squares.*

2 Fold and then unfold the square horizontally.

3 Fold and then unfold the square vertically.

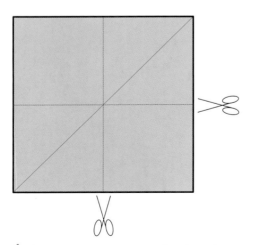

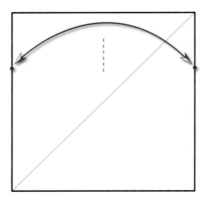

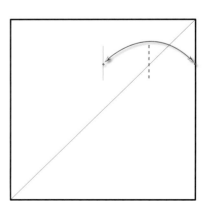

4 Cut your square into quarters. Put three of the quarters into your recycling bin. We will use the remaining square as a measurement tool in step 9. For now set it aside.

5 Using the large square you set aside in step 1, make a small pinch-fold halfway between the left and right edges of your square. We will use this mark as a guide to make the next fold.

6 Make another small pinch-fold halfway between the right edge and the fold you made in step 5. We will use this mark to as a guide to make the next fold.

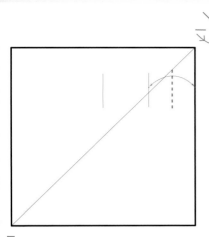

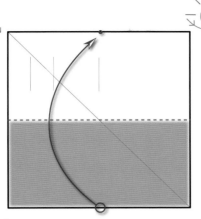

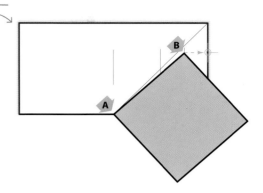

7 Using the fold you made in step 6 as a guide, make a small pinch-fold by folding the right edge toward the center as shown. Flip your square left to right.

8 Fold your square in half horizontally and then flip it left to right.

9 Align one corner of the quarter-size square you made in steps 1 through 4, with point "A" (the intersection of the diagonal and bottom edge). Find point "B" on the fold you made in step 7 as shown. Project the intersection to the outer right edge. Mark the point indicated.

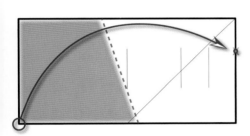

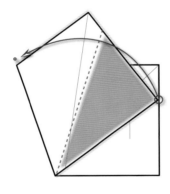

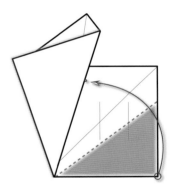

10 Fold the bottom left corner to the point you marked in step 9.

11 Fold the same corner you folded in step 10 up and to the left, aligning the left edge.

12 Fold the bottom right corner up and to the left, aligning it edge to edge.

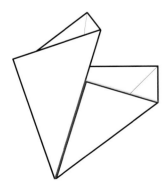

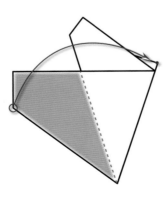

13 Your model should look like this. Flip it left to right.

14 Fold the lower left corner to the rightmost corner.

15 Fold the bottom tip up to the free corner of the top flap.

CUTTING PAPER FOR ORIGAMI IKEBANA

16 Cut as indicated.

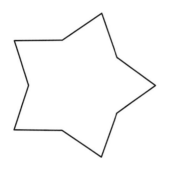

17 Unfold your model and it should look like this. You now have a five-pointed star suitable for folding a five-petal flower.

How to Make Dodecagons for Six Petal Flowers

A dodecagon is a twelve sided figure. You can print dodecagons on your printer using a file named 21-02 dodecagon.png, or you can create them yourself using the instructions which follow.

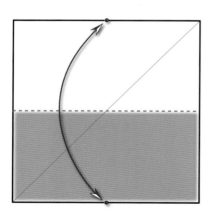

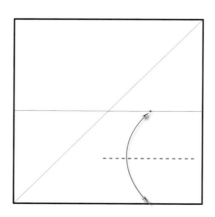

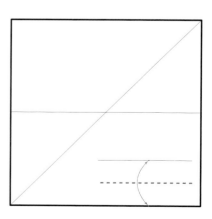

1 Perform steps 1 through 4 of the decagon on page 18. Set aside the small square. Using the large square, fold and unfold your model in half.

2 Using the fold you made in step 1, make a partial fold halfway between it and the bottom edge. Unfold the paper.

3 Use the fold you made in step 2 as a guide to make one more small fold. Unfold the paper.

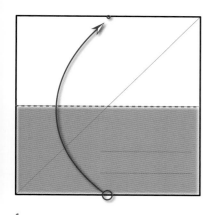

4 Fold your model in half on the fold you made in step 1.

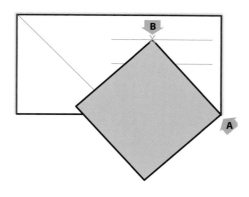

5 Hold one corner of your quarter-size square on point "A" while you find point "B" on the fold you made in step 3. Mark the point, "X" with a pencil.

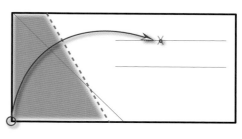

6 Fold the bottom left corner up to the mark you made in step 5.

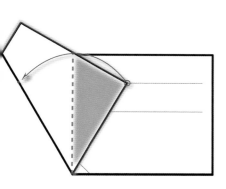

7 Fold the corner you folded in step 6 as shown, carefully aligning the left edge.

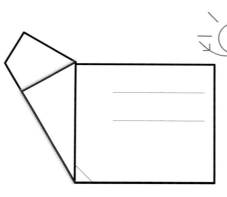

8 Your model should look like this. Flip it left to right.

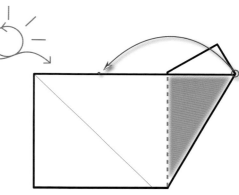

9 Fold the rightmost corner toward the left as shown. This fold should be lined up with the edges of several layers which lie beneath it.

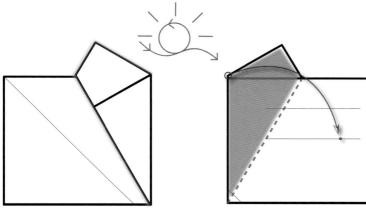

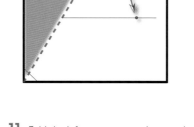

10 Your model should look like this. Flip it left to right.

11 Fold the left upper corner down and to the right. This fold should be lined up with the edges of several layers which lie beneath it.

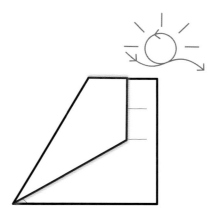

12 Your model should look like this. Flip it left to right.

CUTTING PAPER FOR ORIGAMI IKEBANA

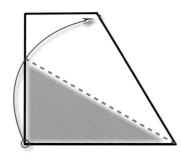

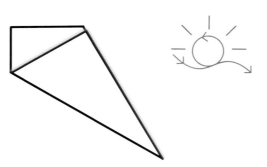

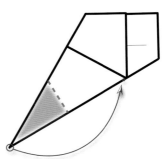

13 Fold the bottom left corner up, aligning the bottom edge to the left edge.

14 Your model should look like this. Flip it left to right.

15 Fold the bottom tip up to a point slightly below the lowest corner, leaving just enough room for the scissors to cut all the layers.

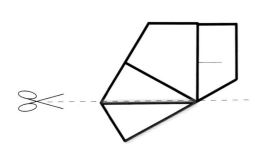

16 Cut along the dashed line as indicated.

17 Unfold your paper and it should look like this (a dodecagon).

INTRODUCTION TO ORIGAMI IKEBANA

Now we venture into an area that I get very excited about. I love to learn something new, and then use that knowledge to expand my abilities. We're going to utilize the Basic Flower Form which you learned to fold on page 44 and we're going to fold over 30 distinct varieties of flower with it.

As you will discover on the pages that follow, each flower has its own unique attributes. Some of these flowers look best when folded in small sizes and some look better in large sizes. Their perspectives vary too. Some look best when they're pointed straight at the viewer, others look nicest when they're pointed slightly away from the viewer. You will also discover that some varieties look dramatically different with five or six petals, and that a few of these flowers are almost impossible to fold with more than four petals.

The information to the right is designed to be a reference tool used in conjunction with the icons that appear next to each new flower project title on the following pages, beginning on page 51. These icons provide information related to painting and folding. They will allow you to maximize the quality, complexity and visual appeal of your finished sculpture. While I strongly recommend that you strictly follow the icon indications for folding, the shaded icons for painting are merely recommendations.

I have had to make several compromises to conserve space and maximize the number of flowers included in this book. Firstly, I will not show five petal icons for shading and folding. The gap when folding should be adjusted in exactly the same way it is for a four petal flower. Shading is the same; however you'll be adding a fifth finger of shade when painting the arced shade pattern. Many of the flower folding instructions include references to other flowers, that means you might want to have a couple of bookmarks available to keep your place.

The order in which the flowers are presented on the following pages is based on their folding characteristics. They are not in order of complexity; in fact, the Curly Michelle, listed early in the series, is one of the hardest flowers to fold successfully.

A note regarding the quality of the paper I made to illustrate the following section of the book: I felt it was important that the paper you see in photos match the color scheme in the diagrams. In the diagrams, one side of the paper is green and the other is yellow. Sadly, preprinted paper that is yellow on one side and green on the other is not widely available. So I had to paint squares specifically for this book. It is almost impossible to paint a light color, like yellow, on one side, and a dark color, like green, on the other, without getting some of the dark color on the light colored side. The pictures in this section bear witness to this. Don't worry about your flowers though. You will use a different painting method (described on page 93).

Project Icon Explanations

When you see this icon it means you should leave a narrow gap (about 1 mm) between petals when performing the fold in step 2 of the Basic Flower Form (page 44). This will allow you to fold the flower without damaging the edges of the petal which will be visible in the final flower.

This icon means you should leave no gap, or even slightly overlap, when performing the folds in step 2 of the Basic Flower Form. We fold in this manner when we're creating a flower with narrow petals and pointy tips. The edges won't be visible in the completed flower, so it's more important that we obtain pointy tips than preserve the inner edges.

Painting a solid shaded area will not emphasize the shadows or shape of this flower.

Painting an arced area of shading will enhance the shape of these flower varieties.

Painting a circle of shading will enhance the shadows created by the center of these varieties of flower.

THE ROTUNDIFOLIUS LEAF

Rotundifolius means "round leaf" in Latin. This folding pattern was inspired by the *Pterocarpus rotundifolius* tree found on the southern portion of the African continent, but you can use it to mimic just about any plant with oval or round leaves. Round leaves are found on many plant species, especially small shrubs. The leaf shape is particularly useful for plants because circular shapes maximize surface area while minimizing the lengths of edges. Consider making your leaves from several differently sized squares, to create a more interesting sculpture.

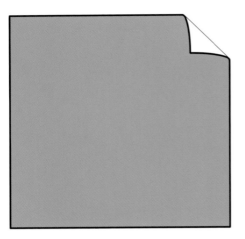

1 Begin with the leaf color facing up.

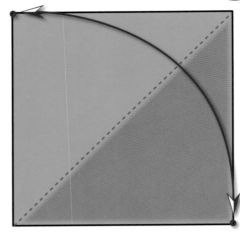

2 Fold and then unfold your square in half diagonally and then flip your square and rotate it 90 degrees.

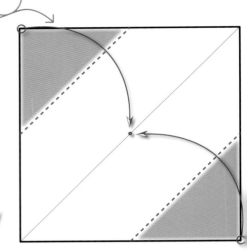

3 Fold the upper left and lower right corners to the center as shown.

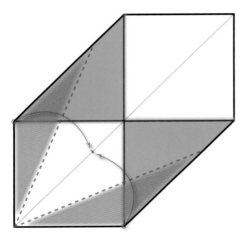

4 Fold the leftmost upper and lowermost right corners to the center as shown.

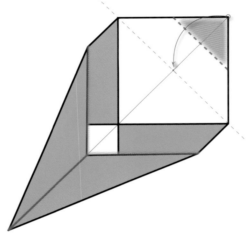

5 Fold the upper right corner down to the indicated level.

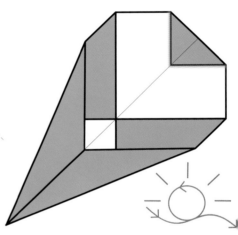

6 Your leaf should look like this. Flip it.

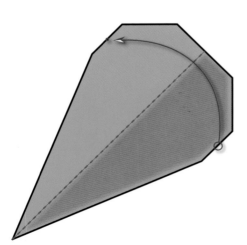

7 Fold the leaf in half on the fold you made in step 2.

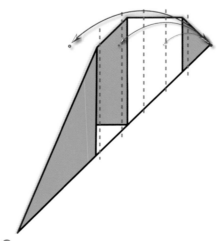

8 Beginning at the rightmost corner, make a small vertical fold and then unfold. Repeat to make a series of parallel, evenly spaced folds. These will represent veins in the finished leaf. The arcs in the diagram show only the first three folds.

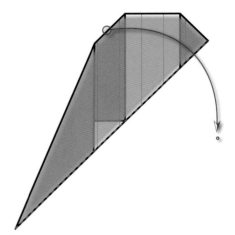

9 Unfold the fold you made in step 7.

10 The leaf should look like this. Flip it.

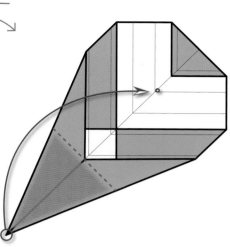

11 Fold the narrow tip up as shown. The fold line is just below the square shape and includes fewer layers of paper. Because of this, you can actually *feel* where this fold is to be made.

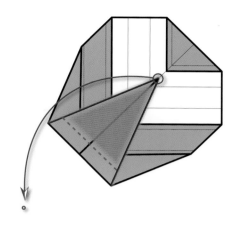

12 Fold the narrow tip down, leaving a gap. If you're not sure where to make this fold, take a look at the next diagram to see where to fold.

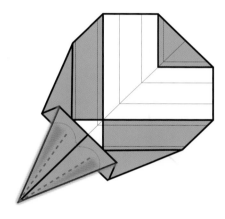

13 Narrow the leaf stem by folding the outer edges in, toward the center fold as shown. Tweezers will be helpful for making this fold.

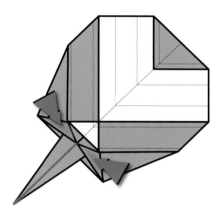

14 Crush-fold the pockets formed by the folds you made in step 13.

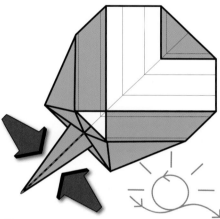

15 Pinch-fold the stem closed. Again, tweezers will be helpful for making this fold. Flip the model to view the top of the completed leaf.

MAKING A NATURAL LOOKING LEAF-STEM CONNECTION

1 Your leaf should look like this.

2 Flatten the leaf–stem connection area by pinching it with your thumb and index finger (my right hand is doing this in the picture).

3 Use your thumbnail to push the flat part of the leaf into the stem on both sides of the fold as shown.

4 Use the flat part of your right hand's thumb, with your index and middle finger supporting the leaf from underneath, and the index finger and thumb of your left hand to crimp the flat area of the leaf into the stem.

5 Your completed leaf should look like this.

THE FICUS LEAF

The round shape we created for the Rotundifolius is quite common in nature. Even more common are oval leaves with points opposite the stem. This leaf, with its pointy tip, looks much like the leaves found on ficus trees and many other plants.

Instead of staining ,these Ficus leaves were painted with thick layers of paint. Notice that the final color isn't as visually complex as the stained and layered finish illustrated on page 96.

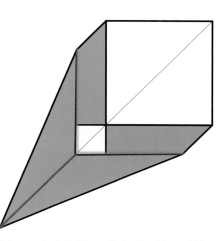

Skip step 5 of the Rotundifolius Leaf (page 26) to fold the Ficus leaf.

Your finished leaf should look like this.

THE BERLIN POPLAR LEAF

This leaf shape is one of the most basic.

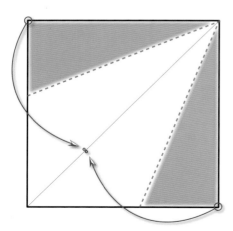

1 Begin by folding steps 1 and 2 of the Rotundifolius on page 26. Fold the top left corner to the center as shown, aligning the top edge with the fold you made in step 2. Do the same with the bottom right corner.

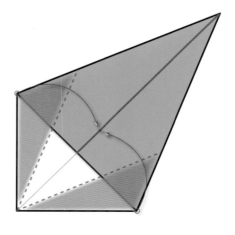

2 Fold the upper left corner to the center, aligning the left edge to the center fold. Do the same with the bottom right corner.

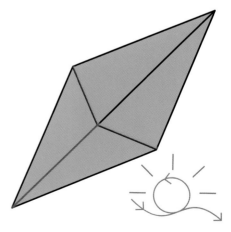

3 Your model should look like this. Flip it.

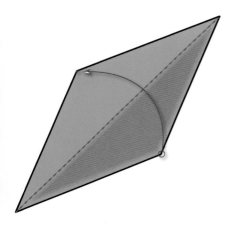

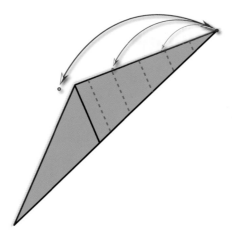

4 Fold the model in half.

5 Beginning at the rightmost corner, make a small fold as shown and then unfold. Repeat to make a series of parallel, evenly spaced folds. These folds will represent veins in the finished leaf. The arcs show only the first three folds.

6 Unfold the fold you made in step 4 and then flip your model.

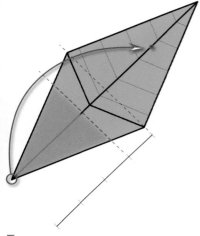

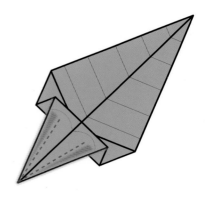

7 Fold the bottom tip up as shown.

8 Fold the same tip back down, leaving a gap. This fold is made at the transition point, where 4 layers of paper become 2 layers, so you can **feel** where it belongs.

9 Narrow the leaf stem by folding the edges in toward the center as shown.

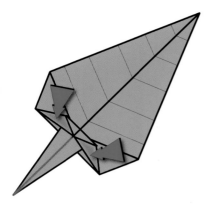

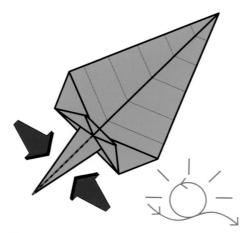

10 Crush-fold the two pockets created by the folds you made in step 9.

11 Pinch-fold the stem closed. Again, tweezers will be helpful for making this fold. Flip the leaf.

12 Follow the instructions on page 28 to create a natural looking leaf-stem connection. Your finished leaf should look like this.

THE IVY LEAF

The Ivy Leaf has a beautiful spade-like shape. This is an attractive leaf which can be used for vines and other plants.

A sculpture made with Ivy Leaves. Notice how the color of the dark leaves contrast with the light lavender color of the Columbine flowers (page 89).

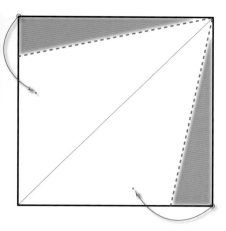

1 Begin by folding steps 1 and 2 of the Rotundifolius on page 26. Fold the top edge down toward the center. Make a similar fold with the right edge.

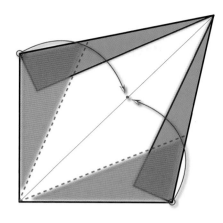

2 Fold the upper left corner down to the center, aligning the left edge with the center fold. Do the same for the bottom right corner.

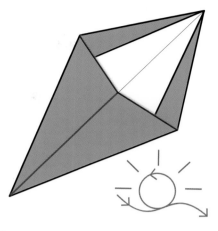

3 Your model should look like this. Flip it.

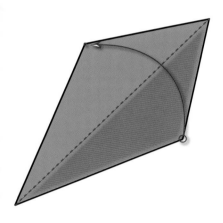

4 Fold your model in half.

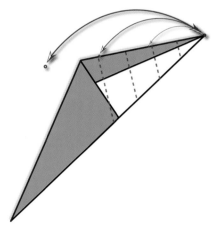

5 Beginning at the rightmost corner, make a small fold and then unfold. Repeat to make a series of parallel, evenly spaced folds. These folds will represent veins in the finished leaf. The arcs show only the first three folds.

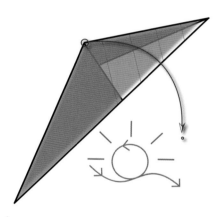

6 Unfold the fold you made in step 4 and flip the model.

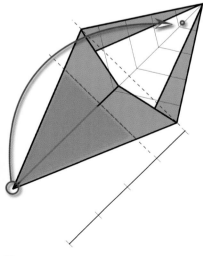

7 Fold the lower left tip up and to the right as shown.

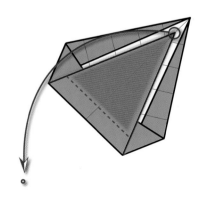

8 Fold the tip back down leaving a gap.

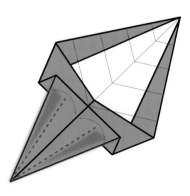

9 Narrow the stem by folding the bottom edges to the center as shown. Tweezers may be helpful.

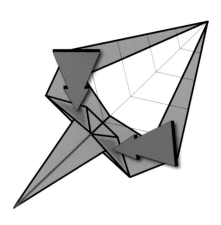

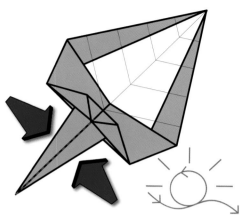

10 Crush-fold the pockets that formed when you made the folds in step 9.

11 Pinch-fold the stem closed. Again, tweezers will be helpful for making this fold. Flip the leaf.

12 Follow the instructions on page 28 to obtain a natural looking leaf–stem connection. Your finished leaf should look like this.

Consider making leaves that vary in both size and shade.

The Boxwood Leaf has a narrow area where the stem connects to the leaf. This makes it possible to attach them in groups of three.

THE BOXWOOD LEAF

This is one of my favorite leaves because it has an interesting shape. The Boxwood Leaf is narrow where the stem connects to the leaf, so it can be attached in pairs, triples, and even sets of 5. You can fold this leaf with a longer or shorter stem by moving the fold in the last step.

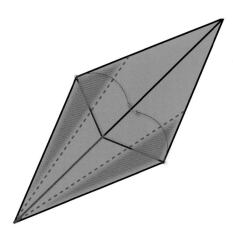

1 Begin by folding steps 1 and 2 of the Berlin Poplar Leaf on page 30. Fold the left edge down toward the center as shown. Make a similar fold with the lower edge.

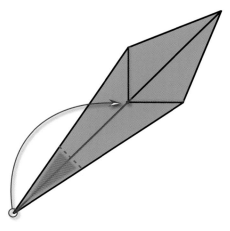

2 Fold the bottom corner up as shown. Perform steps 4 and 5 of the Fern Leaflet (page 39) to complete your leaf.

3 Your completed leaf should look like this.

THE BAMBOO LEAF

The Bamboo Leaf is beautiful, especially when made in several sizes. I find they're most interesting when the size varies greatly. This leaf can present complications at assembly. Because it has a short stem, and a wide stem-leaf connection, when attaching them in pairs, triples or more the stems quickly become a key design consideration.

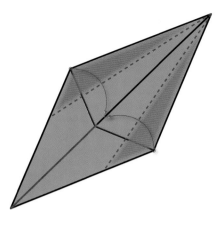

1 Begin by folding steps 1 and 2 of the Berlin Poplar Leaf on page 30. Fold the top edge down toward the center as shown. Make a similar fold with the right edge.

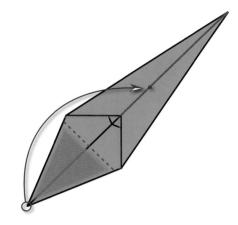

2 Fold the bottom corner up.

3 Fold the tip down, leaving a gap.

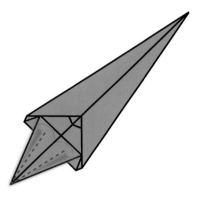

4 Complete the leaf by narrowing the stem as indicated on steps 9–11 for the Berlin Poplar Leaf on page 31.

Notice that the longest leaf was attached so its surface would be parallel to the wall. Smaller leaves were attached at increasing angles pointing toward the wall. This was done to accommodate the Bamboo Leaf's small stems.

Clusters of 5 differently sized Bamboo Leaves add an interesting visual complexity to this sculpture.

5 Your completed leaf should look like this.

Bamboo Leaves.

THE FERN LEAFLET

Fern Leaflets are a challenge to make because, as we narrow our square, our folds must be made on more and more layers of paper. You should have a good, sturdy pair of tweezers to help you make these folds. This leaf size and shape are useful for making plants that have clusters of closely-attached, small leaves, like fern plants.

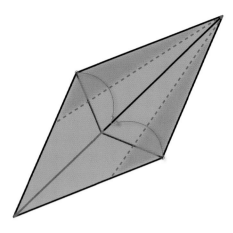

1 Begin by folding steps 1 and 2 of the Berlin Poplar Leaf on page 30. Fold the top left edge toward the center. Make a similar fold with the top right edge.

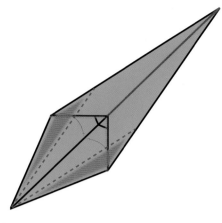

2 Fold the bottom left edge to the center. Do the same with the bottom right edge.

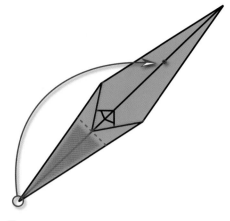

3 Fold the bottom tip up

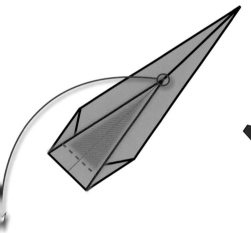

4 Fold the tip back down leaving a gap.

5 Pinch the stem closed, flip it and then follow the instructions on page 28 to obtain a natural looking leaf–stem connection.

6 Your completed Fern Leaflet should look like this.

I keep my leaflets organized in a box with lots of little compartments.

THE MICRO LEAF

Sometimes you'll need to make very small leaves. As the size of our leaves diminishes, it becomes harder to obtain a narrow, good looking stem. This leaf folding pattern is designed with this problem in mind. The stem is created in steps 1 and 2 by a series of folds which resemble rolling, rather than folding, the paper.

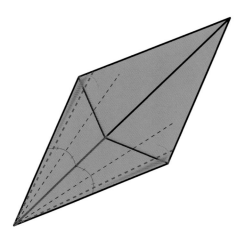

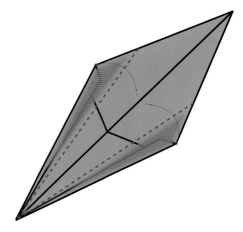

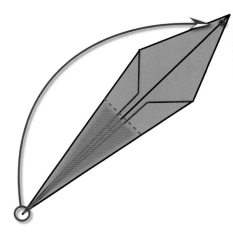

1 Begin by folding steps 1 and 2 of the Berlin Poplar Leaf on page 30. Fold the upper left corner to a point which is less than half way to the center. Do the same with the lower right corner.

2 Fold the upper left corner toward the center leaving a gap. Do the same with the lower right corner.

3 Fold the bottom corner up as shown. Complete your Micro Leaf by doing steps 4 and 5 of the Fern Leaflet on page 39.

The Micro Leaf's folding pattern allows you to make very small leaves.

4 Your completed leaf should look like this.

Black Eyed Susan blossoms can be made from very small squares of paper to make tiny flowers like these.

THE BLACK EYED SUSAN

The Black Eyed Susan is a large, relatively flat flower, which is easy to fold. For people new to folding, this flower offers a good introduction to more complex folding and an even better jumping off point for folding the Basic Flower Form (page 44). When made in larger sizes, this flower can add flare. In small sizes it adds little spots of color for added visual complexity.

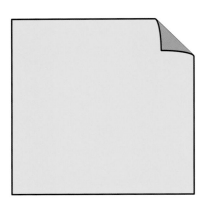

1 Begin with flower color facing up and leaf color facing down.

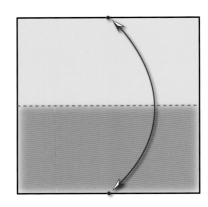

2 Fold and then unfold your square in half horizontally.

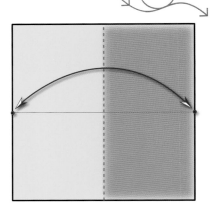

3 Fold and then unfold your square in half vertically. Flip it.

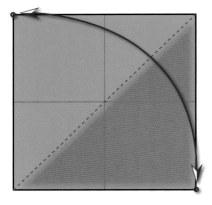

4 Fold and then unfold the square in half diagonally.

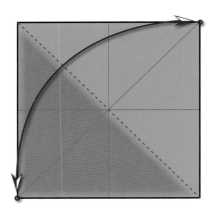

5 Fold and then unfold the square in half diagonally in the other direction.

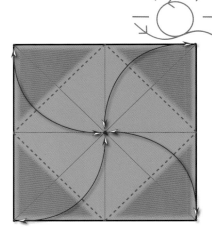

6 Fold and then unfold each corner to the center as shown and then flip the square.

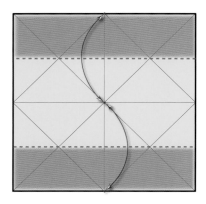

7 Fold and then unfold the top edge to the center. Do the same with the bottom edge.

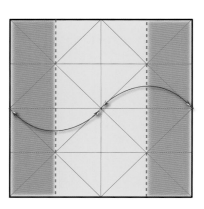

8 Fold and then unfold the left edge to the center. Do the same with the right edge.

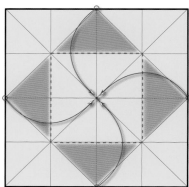

9 Collapse the model by folding the center point of each edge to the center…

10 Just like this. And then...

11 Push each square that gets formed flat.

12 Your model should look like this. Flip it.

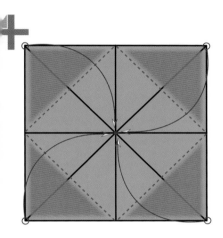

13 Lift your model slightly while folding each corner to the center. Lifting while folding will allow the bottom layer of paper to rotate to the outside of the model.

14 Your model should look like this. Flip it.

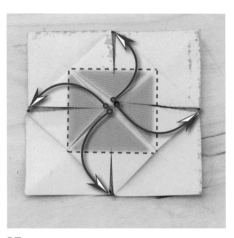

15 The center of the model has four corners. Fold each corner to the outside edge as shown.

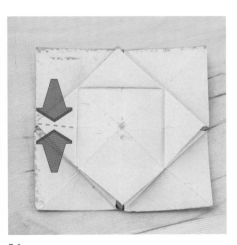

16 Pinch-fold the top layers...

17 By inserting your finger (or a toothpick for smaller flowers) into the pocket. Repeat steps 16 and 17 for the other three pockets.

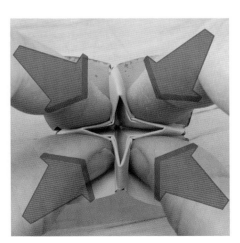

18 Insert a finger deep into each petal and then pinch toward the center to complete the flower.

THE BASIC FLOWER FORM

I first combined folded leaves and flowers with branches in early 2007. At that time I had never developed folding patterns of my own. These early sculptures were impressive mostly because no one had ever seen anything like them before. Sometime in late 2007 I was suffering from a severe case of insomnia. My sister sent me a fantastic origami book. The book included a highly detailed eagle which I really wanted to fold. When my insomnia kept me awake I would work on the eagle. One night I groggily folded, and repeated the same fold on too many sides of the model, performed the next few sequences of folds incorrectly, and ended up with something that looked nothing like the eagle I had set out to fold. However, the shape was remarkable. It reminded me of something; and then I fell asleep.

The next morning I repeated my mistakes and successfully folded the same shape again. I noticed that I could open the edges, and realized that with two-color paper, one color would dominate the outside, and another the inside. I then noticed that I could pinch some of the flaps open. My jaw dropped when I realized what I was holding. It was the first origami flower I had seen that looked real. Today I call this shape the basic flower form, and since 2007 I have developed 30 distinct flowers from it.

In 2011 I discovered that the basic flower form's folding pattern worked with any number of petals. I developed a method for folding it using templates and a glass cutting tool. As I saw tremendous utility in the folding pattern, I filed for a patent for it (US patent number 8,545,286). A few weeks later I was contacted by Tanya Duffy of Australia. She claimed she had discovered a way to fold flowers with any number of petals. I investigated her claim and discovered that the folding pattern followed an elegantly simple rule. The basic flower form can be folded with any number of petals so long as the shape of the material to be folded is made up of congruent diamond-shapes distributed about a center point, with each diamond being made up of two congruent triangles.

Flowers with four petals can easily be made using a square piece of paper, however flowers with 3, 5, and 6 petals are a little harder to make. I have provided several templates on the DVD which accompanies this book. If you do not have access to a computer and printer, there are also instructions on pages 18–22 for cutting pieces of paper suitable for 3, 5 and 6 petal flowers.

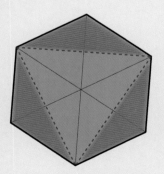

This hexagon will make a three petal flower.

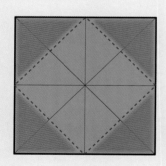

A square will make a four petal flower.

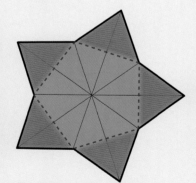

This decagon will make a five petal flower.

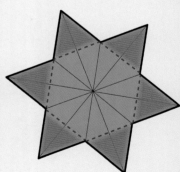

A dodecagon will make a six petal flower.

Opening the flaps of a four petal (made from a square piece of paper) **basic flower form** creates the **Michelle** flower (page 51).

FOLDING THE BASIC FLOWER FORM FOR AN EVEN NUMBER OF PETALS

As mentioned, the Basic Flower Form can be folded from any shape that will support its need for congruent diamond-shapes. Flowers with an even petal count are a little bit easier to fold than those with odd. What follows is the basic flower folding pattern at it simplest, using a square piece of paper to make a four-petal flower.

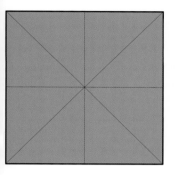

1 Begin by folding the black eyed Susan on page 42 up to and including step 5.

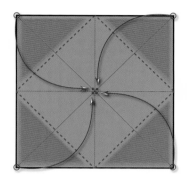

2 Fold each corner to the center as shown, leaving a gap. For now just leave a small gap, but in the future, the gap will be determined by the flower you plan to produce.

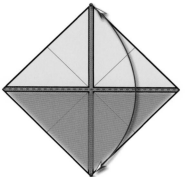

3 Fold and then unfold your model in half horizontally.

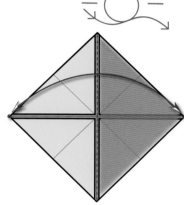

4 Fold and then unfold your model in half vertically and then flip it.

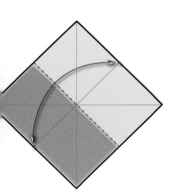

5 Fold and then unfold your model in half as shown.

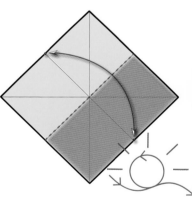

6 Fold and then unfold your model in half as shown and then flip your model.

7 Push each corner toward the center. Allow the center to rise like a tent.

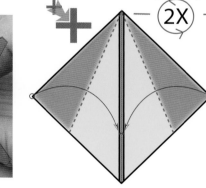

8 Fold the upper layers of paper to the center as shown. Flip your model and do the same on the other side.

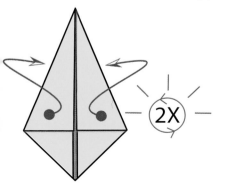

9 Inside-reverse-fold all four of the flaps you created in step 8. Refer to steps 10—14 for details.

10 A sharp fold reverses easily. To perform an inside-reverse-fold, first sharpen the folds to be reversed by sliding your fingernail down them. I also often use a wallpaper seam rolling tool to do this.

Hint: To avoid blemishes on your flower petals, sharpen your folds on top of a fresh, clean sheet of paper.

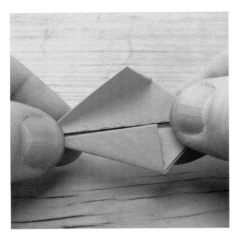

11 Open one of the folds you made in step 8.

12 Insert your index finger to open the flap.

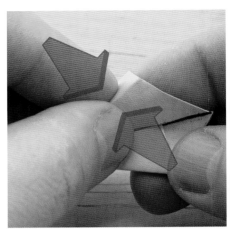

13 Pinch-fold the closer, outer fold to reverse its direction.

14 Push the inner fold toward the center of the model. Close the flap and repeat steps 11 through 14 on the next flap.

15 When you have reversed all 4 flaps your model should look like this.

16 Gather the edges and then book-fold your model so it looks like this.

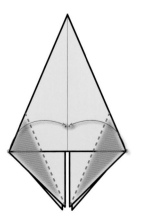

17 Fold the outside corners of the upper layers of paper so that they slightly overlap.

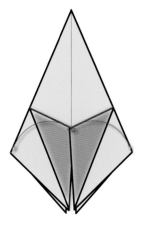

18 Unfold the folds you made in step 17.

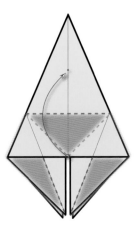

19 Fold the point indicated upwards and then crush-fold flat. The mountain folds depicted will be made automatically.

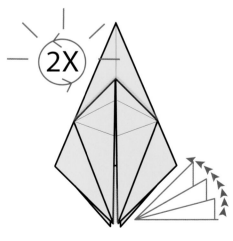

20 Your model should look like this. Unfold the folds you made in step 19. Repeat these folds on the other side, then book-fold and repeat on the two inner sides. (See tip on opposite page.)

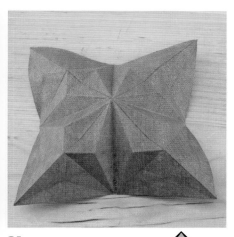

21 Completely unfold your model. Orient it so that the leaf color is facing up (as shown). Collapse the square.

22 Pinch the flaps on two opposite sides and push toward the center to begin the collapse.

23 Now pinch the flaps on the other two sides and push toward the center.

24 Push the flaps all the way into the center of the model and then pinch the folds so they close tightly.

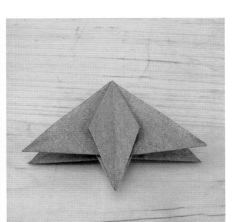

25 Book-fold your model so there is an even number of layers of paper on both sides.

Now you're ready to try the Michelle on page 51.

A Tip: You can skip steps 17 and 18 by lifting the center of the flap as shown.

B Pinch and then push or pull the edges of the flap to adjust the horizontal fold line (in step 19).

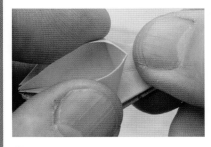

C Squeeze the sides closed.

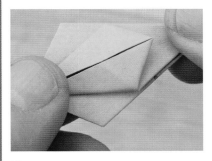

D Crush and pinch the folds into place. This technique takes a little practice, but it will save you a lot of time.

FOLDING THE BASIC FLOWER FORM FOR AN ODD NUMBER OF PETALS

I began this section showing how to fold a four petal Basic Flower Form from a square for several reasons; the square represents traditional origami, square pieces of origami paper are easy to obtain, diagrams based on squares are familiar to folding enthusiasts. If you have not yet folded a Basic Flower Form with four petals I urge you to back up a few pages and fold one. Your success at folding a flower with an odd number of petals increases greatly if you first fold a flower with four petals.

It is important to note that the advantages to folding a square become disadvantages when folding shapes that are not square. Merely obtaining a piece of paper in the proper shape can be a challenge. For three and five petal flowers we use a hexagon and decagon respectively. I opted not to show the three petal flower in this demonstration because the final flower shape looks odd. Instead, I'll show you the folding pattern based on five petals. You will notice that we achieve amazingly real looking flowers. One reason the five petal flower looks real to us is because many large, cultivated flowers have five petals.

Because we are dealing with a more complex shape, I need to communicate clearly with language you will understand. We have two types of folds, mountains and valleys. I shall now also refer to peaks and dales. Peaks are the outer corners, or tips of the shapes we're dealing with. Dales are the inner corners, or valleys of the shapes.

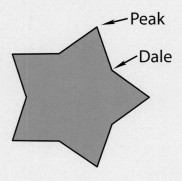

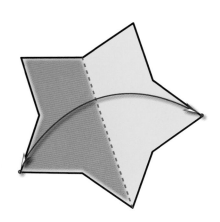

1 Begin by making a decagon either by printing a template from the DVD or by using the cutting instructions on page 19. Begin with the flower side facing up. Fold and then unfold between one dale and one peak.

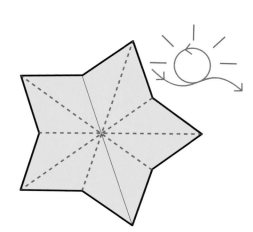

2 Fold just as you did in step 1 between all the peaks and dales. After making these folds, flip your paper.

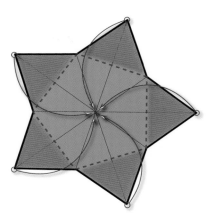

3 Before folding, look at the diagram in step 4. Fold each peak to the center as shown, but leave a narrow gap between the edges.

4 Your model should look like this.

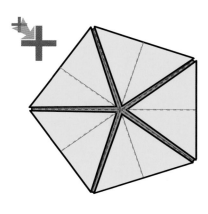

5 Change the directions of the folds as shown. The folds inside the gaps will be valley folds, in the middle of the petals will be mountain folds.

6 Your model should look like this. Notice that this image looks similar to step 7 on page 95, but with 5 sides instead of four. Notice that the folds affecting each petal are exactly the same. Collapse the model.

7 Your model should look like this. It will have more layers of paper on one side than the other.

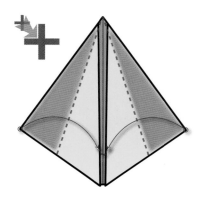

8 Fold the outer corners of the top layers of paper to the center as shown.

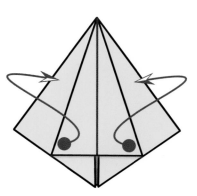

9 Inside-reverse-fold the folds you made in step 8. See steps 10 through 14 on pages 45 and 46 if you become confused.

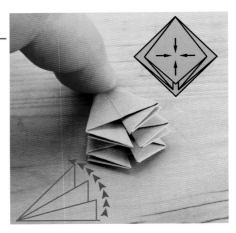

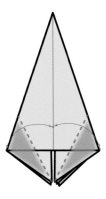

10 Flip your model and repeat steps 8 and 9 on the opposite side, and then book-fold and repeat on the final, hidden side. Your model should look like this.

11 Collapse and then book-fold your model until it looks like this.

12 Fold and then unfold the outer corners to a point just barely beyond the center line as shown.

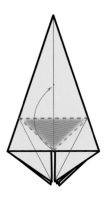

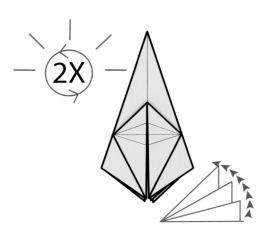

13 Fold the point indicated upwards and then crush-fold flat just as you did in step 19 on page 46. The mountain folds depicted will be made automatically.

14 Your model should look like this. Unfold the folds you made in step 13. Repeat these folds on the other side, then book-fold and repeat on the three inner sides.

15 Completely unfold your model. It should look like this.

16 Collapse a petal to exercise its folds, and then uncollapse it. Repeat on all five petals.

17 Collapse each petal to the center just as you did in steps 21 through 25 on page 47.

18 Your model should look like this.

THE MICHELLE

The Michelle is a dramatic, but delicate flower, with long gentle curves, but be forewarned, it may lose some of its character over time. This flower will react to changes in humidity and temperature by slowly closing back into the Basic Flower Form. If you're planning to use this flower in a sculpture I urge you to use extra artist's medium in your final coat of paint. This will help prevent petal migration over time.

1 Begin with the Basic Flower Form (page 45). Separate each petal (the longer flaps) and distribute the layers of paper evenly as shown. Notice that each petal has two corresponding smaller flaps.

2 Insert your index fingers into two opposing petals. Pinch the inner corners flat as shown.

3 Carefully repeat step 2 on the other two petals. You may find that one petal collapses as you do this. If that happens, try pinching and pulling the petals outwards simultaneously.

THE CURLY MICHELLE

I think this is one of the most beautiful flowers that can be created from the Basic Flower Form. It has many long, luxurious curves along with a pointy center. Interestingly, I didn't discover how to curl the petals for more than two years after I discovered the Basic Flower Form's folding pattern. This flower is among the more challenging to fold successfully. I urge you to practice folding this flower before designing a sculpture based upon it.

1 Begin with the Basic Flower Form (page 45). Open a petal and then pull it down until it forms a flat plane as shown.

2 Reorient your model as shown, putting your index fingers under the petal and your thumbs on top of it. **Gently and carefully** curl the petal over your index fingers. Be careful not to rip the edges of the petal. Repeat steps 1 and 2 on the other petals.

THE PRIMROSE

I love this flower in part because it was one if the first I discovered, but also because it looks so much like a real flower. A four-petal Primrose looks lovely, and a five-petal looks even better. A quarter-size Primrose is used as the center flower in the Columbine Assembly you'll find on page 92.

1 The upper tip of the Basic Flower Form (page 45) is made up of four tips. Fold the uppermost tip down, as far as it will go. Notice that it will not go all the way to the bottom of the bud.

2 Fold up the tip that you folded down in step 1, coming to rest just barely below the crease you made in step 1.

3 Your model should look like this. Flip it and perform the folds in step 1 and 2 on the opposite side, then book-fold it and perform the steps on the two inner tips.

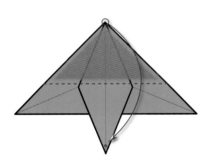

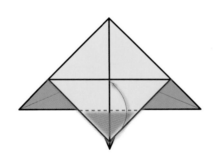

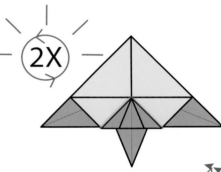

4 Separate the petals.

5 Open a petal from underneath and push it up as shown. Repeat on all four petals.

THE THISTLE

The Thistle is the same as the Primrose except that it has pointy tips that emerge from the center of the flower. These tips look like stamens. These tips change the geometry of the Primrose; a useful addition to larger sized flowers.

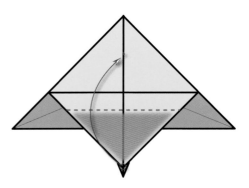

Begin with the Basic Flower Form (page 45). Follow the instructions for folding the Primrose on page 54, but in step 2, fold the bottom tip up leaving a small gap instead of folding it up to the fold.

THE BUD

The Bud is one of my favorite flowers. I like to make some buds that are approximately 1/3 the size of the open flowers I'm making for a sculpture. My finished sculpture will have both open flowers and much smaller buds, thus evoking a feeling of transition and growth.

1 Begin with the Basic Flower Form (page 45). Follow the instructions for folding the Primrose on page 55, up to step 4. Open a petal (like you did for the Primrose) and then push it all the way into the center of the flower.

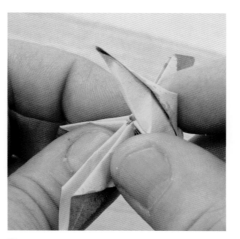

2 Squeeze the edges of the petal closed as shown to form a hollow, tapered shaft. Repeat steps 1 and 2 on the other three petals.

These buds were made about one-third smaller than the five petal Primrose on this sculpture.

THE PHLOX

The Phlox is another derivative of the Primrose. It has cute, curly petals. Try making it in larger sizes and then add long, luxurious stamens for an interesting finished look.

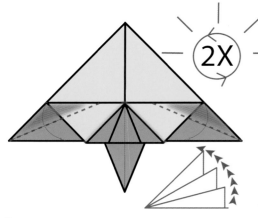

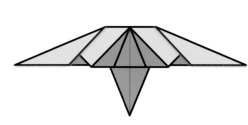

1 Begin with the Basic Flower Form (page 45). Fold the Primrose on page 53 up to step 3. Fold the corners of the top edges of the top layer of paper down on the existing fold as shown. Flip your model and repeat on the other side, then book-fold and repeat on the two hidden sides.

2 After folding all four petals, a total of eight edges, your model should look like this. Separate the petals as you did with the Primrose.

3 Use both hands to open the petal. Put your thumbs into the crevice and then use your index fingers to hold the flaps you folded in step 3 in place. Gently push from underneath the petal and...

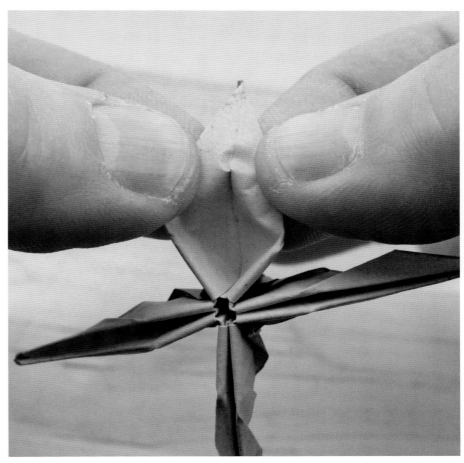

4 Rotate your hands so that the petal curls. Repeat steps 3 and 4 on the other four petals.

5 Shape each petal by pulling it down.

THE PHLOX WITH STAMENS

The Phlox with stamens is a slight modification of the Phlox.

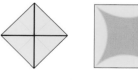

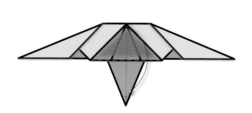

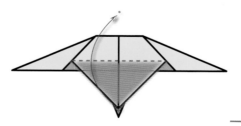

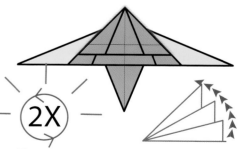

1 Begin with the Basic Flower Form (page 45). Fold the Phlox on page 56 up to step 2 and then unfold the fold you made in step 2 of the Primrose.

2 Fold the corner back up creating a new fold just below the flaps you made in step 1 of the Phlox.

3 Flip your model and repeat steps 1 and 2 on the other side, and then book-fold and repeat on the two hidden sides. Open and shape the flower as you did with the Phlox on page 57.

THE IPECAC

This flower has an interesting geometric shape. When I have some spare time I'd like to make a sculpture featuring these flowers. I'd orient them so that each flower directly faces the viewer.

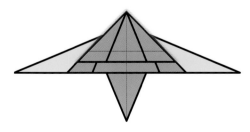

Begin with the Basic Flower Form (page 45). Fold the Phlox with Stamens on the opposite page, but open it by following the Buttercup steps 3 through 5 on page 64.

THE BANANA

I think this is a really cute flower. It's got a narrow center hole, but instead of petals that curl down, these curl out and up. This flower is especially good-looking when made in smaller sizes.

Several Banana flowers in a luscious shade of peach.

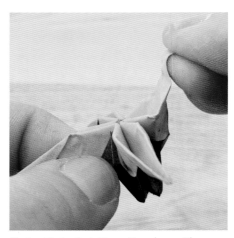 

Begin with the Basic Flower Form (page 45). Folding is identical to the Phlox on page 56. Once folded, instead of curling the petals down, pull them up.

THE BANANA WITH STAMENS

This is another derivation, but this time of the Phlox with stamens.

Begin with the Basic Flower Form (page 45). Fold the Phlox with stamens on page 58, but instead of curling each petal down, pull them up as you did with the Banana flower on the opposite page.

THE FLEUR DE LIS

The Fleur de Lis is
another Phlox derivative
and can be created with
or without stamens.

Begin with the Basic Flower Form (page 45). Fold
the Phlox on page 56, but instead of curling the
petals, lift the flaps you folded in step 1.

THE BUTTERCUP

This is an easy flower to fold.

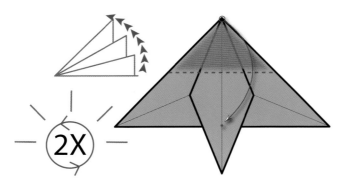

1 Begin with the Basic Flower Form (page 45). Fold the upper tip of the top layer of paper down as shown. Flip your model and repeat on the other side, then book-fold and repeat on the two hidden sides.

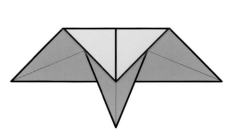

2 Your model should look like this.

3 Insert your finger into one of the petals to open it and then...

4 Align the center fold and crush-fold it flat. Flip it and repeat steps 3 and 4 to the petal on the opposite side, then book-fold and repeat on the two hidden petals.

5 Your model should look like this. Pull each petal down and your Buttercup will be complete.

THE PUMPKIN FLOWER

I discovered this variant of the Buttercup while writing this book. The Pumpkin Flower can also be used instead of the Primrose when making Columbine flower assemblies.

1 Begin with the Basic Flower Form (page 45). Fold the Buttercup on page 63. After you've opened the petals, push up underneath each petal with your index finger as shown. Allow the petal to develop a curl.

2 After opening all four petals, pull opposing petals down to shape the flower.

THE MORNING GLORY

This flower is rapidly becoming one of my favorites. It has an interesting shape, and lots of surface area where I can add embellishments, like color changes. There's also a generous amount of space in the center for adding long, curved makigami stamens (see page 110). Curved stamens contrast with the flat petal surfaces, creating a visually impressive display. Even though the shading icon to the right suggests you paint no shading, the Morning Glory's wide petals offer space for experimentation.

Opening the Morning Glory can be a challenge. You'll find that the paper needs to be stretched a bit because there isn't enough room for the wide petals at the center of the flower. Because of this, the five and six petal versions of this flower have overlapping petals.

If you have trouble opening the petals, try folding the Posey (page 77) instead. The shape is similar to the Morning Glory, but it's a lot easier to open.

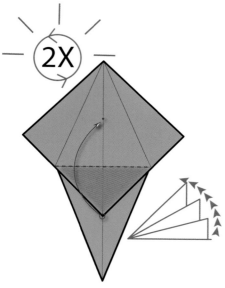

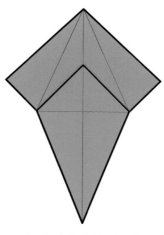

1 Begin with the Basic Flower Form (page 45). Perform steps 1 through 4 of the Buttercup on page 63 so your model looks like this. Fold the flap up as shown on the existing fold. Repeat on the opposite side, book-fold and repeat on the two hidden sides.

2 Your model should look like this. Open the flower by pulling the tip of each petal down (see next step).

3 You will find that you can easily open three petals, but the fourth wants to close. Use your fingertips to stretch the paper a bit, opening opposite petals and then…

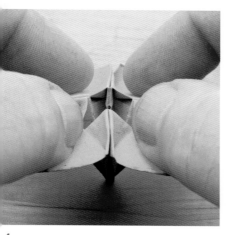

4 Put the tip of the bud on a surface and lightly push all four petals down.

5 Curl the tips of the petals down, toward the bud.

THE MORNING GLORY WITH STAMENS

If you don't plan to make stamens from makigami, here's a way to add origami stamens to the Morning Glory flower. The stamens look nice because they help break up the flat surface of the flower.

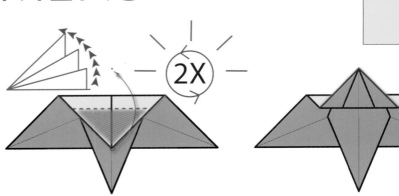

1 Begin with the Basic Flower Form (page 45). Fold the Buttercup on page 63 up to step 2. Now fold the tip back up, leaving a small gap as shown. Flip your model and repeat on the other side, and then book-fold and repeat on the two hidden sides.

2 Your model should look like this. Now fold it beginning with step 1 of the Morning Glory on page 67.

THE SHORT SHOOTING STAR

This is an interesting little flower. Because it is semi-collapsed in its final shape, it appears smaller than other flowers. Because both sides of the petals are visible from any direction, this flower presents an opportunity to do interesting things with color, like painting the petals a different color on the top and bottom sides.

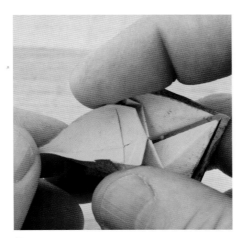

1 Begin with the Basic Flower Form (page 45). Fold the Morning Glory on page 66 through step 2. Open one petal at a time by rotating the tip all the way down to the bud as shown.

2 Squeeze the petal closed as shown. Repeat steps 1 and 2 on all four petals to complete the flower.

THE BUNCHBERRY

**This flower is a simple modification
of the Short Shooting Star.**

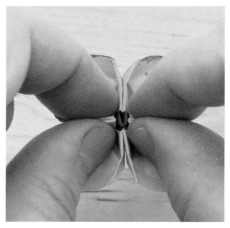

Begin with the Basic Flower Form (page 45). Fold
the Short Shooting Star on page 69 and then
insert your fingers and push toward the center as
shown, expanding the petals a bit.

THE TRILLIUM

This is a useful flower with luxurious, wide and curly petals that looks great from any angle. I love how shading interacts with the shape of the flower, making it look more complex than it really is.

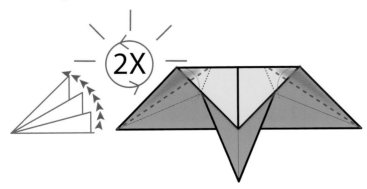

1 Begin with the Basic Flower Form (page 45). Fold the Buttercup on page 63 up to step 2. Fold the edges of the top layer down as shown. Flip your model and repeat on the opposite side, and then book-fold and repeat on the two hidden sides.

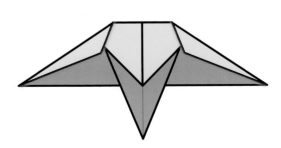

2 Your model should look like this. Open each petal by curling it just as you did the Curly Michelle on page 52.

THE HIPPEASTRUM

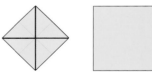

This flower has tremendous potential. It has an interesting shape, and has petals that jut away from the center rather than bending back. There's also plenty of room for makigami stamens in the center.

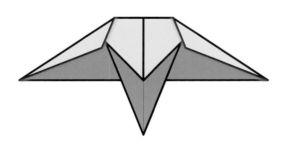

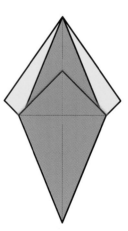

1 Begin with the Basic Flower Form (page 45). Fold the Trillium on page 71 up to step 2. Push each petal up as you did in steps 3, 4, and 5 of the Buttercup on page 64, then fold the little flaps up just as you did while folding step 1 of the Morning Glory on page 67.

2 Your model should look like this. Follow the Morning Glory's instructions on page 67 when opening the petals.

THE SCORPION WEED

This is an interesting and different flower design. After the final step you can choose to leave the petals with a straight, rigid look, or curve them for a softer look.

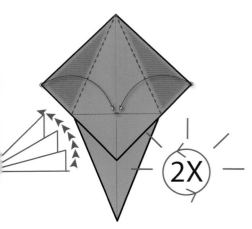

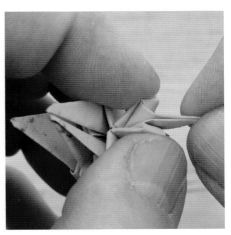

1 Begin with the Basic Flower Form (page 45). Fold the Buttercup on page 64 and then fold the edges in as shown. Flip your model and repeat on the other side, then book-fold and repeat on the hidden sides.

2 Pull a petal down as shown.

3 Pinch the base of the petal (as I'm doing with my left hand) while you pull the petal down (as I'm doing with my right hand). Repeat steps 2 and 3 on the other petals.

The Clematis is a nice flower. It has an interesting shape and can be made in very small sizes. I like to attach Clematis flowers at interesting angles. This tends to show off the bud connection and underside of the flower which I think are interesting to look at.

THE CLEMATIS

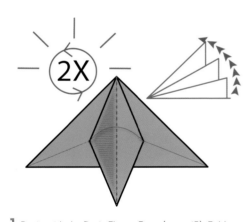

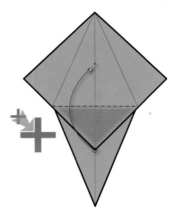

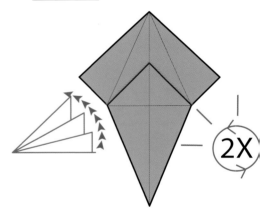

1 Begin with the Basic Flower Form (page 45). Fold the top layer of paper to the right. Insert your finger into the petal and fold the area flat just as you did with the Buttercup on page 63. Flip your model and do the same on the other side, and then book-fold your model and do the same on the two hidden sides.

2 Fold the small flap up on the existing fold.

3 Your model should look like this. Flip it and repeat step 2 on the opposite side, then book-fold it and repeat on the two hidden sides. Open the flower just as you did the Morning Glory on page 67.

These tiny Clematis flowers are only partially open.

I stumbled upon this flower after I folded my first Michelle flower and then forgot that it existed. I rediscovered it a couple years later and built a beautiful sculpture using a cluster of them. Make sure you use extra artist's medium in your final coat of paint as this flower's petals tend to migrate a bit over time.

THE DRAGON HEAD

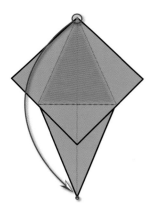 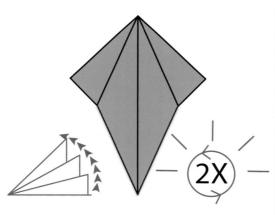 

1 Begin with the Basic Flower Form (page 45). Fold the Buttercup on page 63 up to step 5. Then fold the top corner down on the existing horizontal fold as shown. The two mountain folds will be created automatically from existing folds.

2 Your model should like this. Flip your model and repeat step 1 on the other side, then book-fold and repeat on the two hidden sides.

3 Pull each petal out; they'll kind of pop once completely extended.

 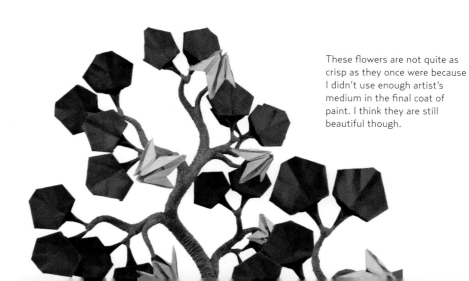

4 Pinch the edges as shown where the petal connects to the flower. In this picture, my right hand is doing the pinching; my left hand is just holding the flower. Repeat on each petal.

These flowers are not quite as crisp as they once were because I didn't use enough artist's medium in the final coat of paint. I think they are still beautiful though.

THE SOLANUM

The Solanum is a simple modification you can make to the Dragon's Head.

Begin with the Basic Flower Form (page 45). Fold the Dragon Head on page 75 and then open each petal.

THE POSEY

This flower is similar to the Morning Glory, but with larger protrusions in its center. It's folding pattern was developed in response to stiffer papers which made it almost impossible to open the Morning Glory. This folding pattern resolves the opening problem.

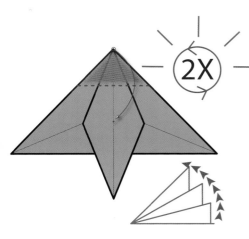

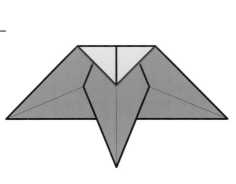

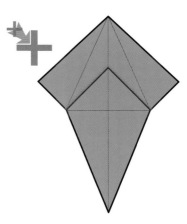

1 Begin with the Basic Flower Form (page 45). Fold the top layers of the tip down as shown. Flip your model and repeat on the other side, then book-fold and repeat on the two hidden sides.

2 Your model should look like this. Do steps 2 through 5 of the Buttercup on page 63, and then steps 1 and 2 of the Morning Glory on page 67.

3 Your model should look like this. Open it just as you did the Morning Glory on page 67.

THE LONG SHOOTING STAR

This is a little more dramatic version of the Short Shooting Star.

1 Begin with the Basic Flower Form (page 45). Fold the Posey on page 77 and then fold each of the little flaps on the bottom down toward the bud.

2 Pinch the petals closed just as you did with the Short Shooting Star on page 69.

THE PYROLA

This flower is similar to the Buttercup but has narrower petals and bolder lines.

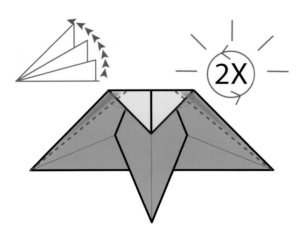

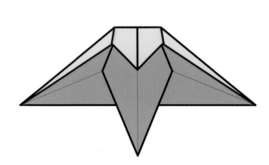

1 Begin with the Basic Flower Form (page 45). Fold the Posey on page 77 to step 2, then fold the edges down as shown. Flip your model and fold the edges down on the other side and then book-fold and repeat on the two hidden sides.

2 Your model should look like this. To open it, follow the instructions for the Buttercup on page 64 beginning on step 3.

THE CRANESBILL

This flower has bold, crisp lines and sharply cornered petals.

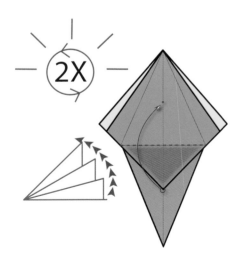

1 Begin with the Basic Flower Form (page 45). Fold the Pyrola on page 79 up to step 2, but don't open it. Your model should look like this. Fold the flap up as shown, flip it and do the same on the opposite side, then book-fold and repeat on the two hidden sides.

2 Open the flower just as you did the Morning Glory on page 67. Five and six-petal varieties can be a challenge to open.

THE SNAP DRAGON

This is a flower that, time permitting, I will investigate further. I believe it has tremendous potential. Notice its streamlined shapes and elegant lines. I suspect this flower will appear in several of my sculptures in the future.

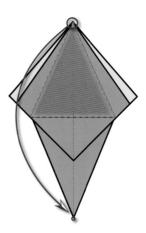

Begin with the Basic Flower Form (page 45). Fold the Pyrola on page 79 up to step 2—but don't open it. Your model should look like this. Fold the top corner of the top layers of paper down on the existing fold. Pinch the mountain folds into place on the existing folds. Flip and repeat on the opposite side, then book-fold and repeat on the two hidden sides.

THE DROOPY

When folded properly, the Droopy is a luscious flower. It has gracefully curved petals and looks especially beautiful when made with five and six petals.

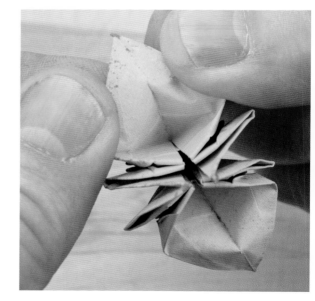

Begin with the Basic Flower Form (page 45). Fold the Pyrola on page 79 up to step 2—but don't open it. Open the petals by curling them around your index fingers just as you did with the Curly Michelle on page 52.

THE FOXGLOVE

This is an interesting flower that I discovered several years ago while riding as a passenger in a car. I have used it in many sculptures.

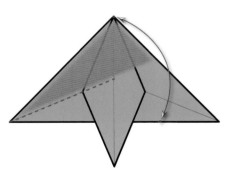

1 Begin with the Basic Flower Form (page 45). Fold and then unfold the left edge of the top layers as shown, scoring the fold only to the center and not beyond.

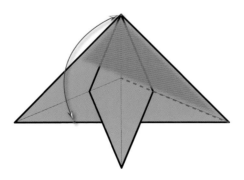

2 Fold and then unfold the right edge of the top layers as shown, scoring the fold only to the center not beyond.

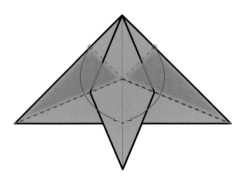

3 Now bring both edges down simultaneously...

4 Like this, and then…

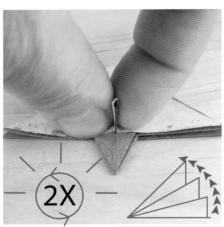

5 Pinch the little flap closed. Flip your model and repeat steps 1 through 5 on the other side, then book–fold it and repeat again on the two hidden sides.

6 Separate the petals and then open them by pushing up from underneath.

THE DAISY

This is one of my favorite flowers. You will find it on many of my sculptures.

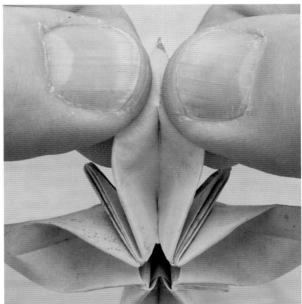

Begin with the Basic Flower Form (page 45). Fold the Foxglove on page 83. Place your index fingers under, and your thumbs over one of the petals. Add a curve to it by moving your hands slightly closer together. Repeat on the other petals.

THE COROLLA

This is an interesting flower that I have used in several sculptures. I also like to paint leaf-colored Corolla's and use them to represent foliage.

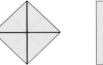

1 Fold the Foxglove on page 83 up to step 5. Open each petal by unfolding the two edges underneath and then...

2 Push up from underneath to pop the petals into a downward-angled configuration.

THE LADY SLIPPER

I rediscovered this flower while writing this book. This is a beautiful flower which is fairly difficult to fold. Be a little careful when curling the petals as it is possible to tear your flower. The procedure is shown on the following page.

1 Begin with the Basic Flower Form (page 45). Separate and then pull out one of the petals to unfold it.

2 Pinch the petal to flatten its surface.

3 Turn the edges of the petal inside out by curling them over your fingers as shown. This will feel a little risky. If it seems like your paper will tear, you didn't flatten enough in step 2.

4 Push the petal toward the center of the flower so the inner folds return to their original position.

5 The petal should look like this. Repeat on the other three petals.

USING FLOWERS IN ASSEMBLIES

As you've seen on the previous pages, the basic flower form is a highly versatile origami shape. In many respects however, that may be just the beginning. Flowers of different sizes can be combined to create new flowers. They can also be combined to create leaves for small shrubs.

While we are unable to "grow" a flower within a flower, we can produce assemblies of flowers. Pictured on the following pages are several assemblies I've developed. There are probably an infinite number of assemblies which can be produced for origami ikebana. I encourage you to explore these possibilities and share your discoveries with other origami ikebana enthusiasts.

I used flowers to represent foliage for these chess pieces. Notice the "queen" (left) has three flowers for leaves and a flower assembly—including a bud—for her crown.

Here is a Double-Dip flower made by combining red Trillium flowers (page 71) mounted on a cream Daisy (page 85).

This Columbine flower (page 92) was painted using the **silk technique** which is described in my first book, **Origami Bonsai** (Tuttle Publishing, 2010).

Each of these flower assemblies are made up of four flowers; three Long Shooting Stars (page 78) and one Bud (page 55). There may be hundreds of different flower combinations that can be created with flower assemblies.

These five-petal Columbine flowers (page 92) are particularly beautiful. Notice that the outer, red flower has a glossy finish, while the inner, white flower is matte.

Clusters of flowers are common in nature. I believe that plants which produce smaller flowers have found a way to compete with those that produce larger flowers. They do so by combining flowers into clusters, or flowers within flowers. A pollinator probably finds a large flower more attractive than a small one; however, it might also find a cluster of five flowers more attractive than a single large flower.

THE COLUMBINE FLOWER ASSEMBLY

I think this is my favorite assembly. I've used it on sculptures for many years and still love the way the flowers seem to interact with each other. I especially like the look achieved with the five-petal variety.

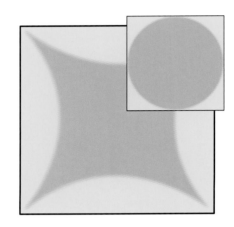

Cut one large square and paint and fold it as a Daisy (page 85). Cut a second square one quarter the size of the first and fold it as a Primrose (page 53). Insert and then glue the Primrose to the center of the Daisy.

THE DOUBLE DIP FLOWER ASSEMBLY

This is a relatively new flower assembly that I have yet to fully explore. The Double Dip flower assembly allows us to explore both color and shape in dramatic and different ways. The combination of a spherical four-flower assembly and a large, droopy flower combine to form a flower that looks a little bit like a dripping ball of ice cream on a hot day. When creating these assemblies, consider using highly contrasting colors. Combine a pink sphere with a dark blue drooping flower, or a black droop with a white or pink sphere. These combinations are sure to delight viewers.

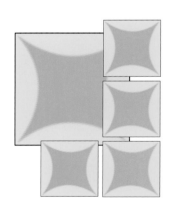

Cut one large square and paint and fold it as a Daisy (page 85). Cut four squares one quarter the size of the first and fold them as Trilliums (page 71). Insert the bud of each Trillium into the center of each petal of the Daisy and glue it in place.

PAINTING LEAVES AND FLOWERS

In some respects this might be the most important section in this book. That's because for many people, color is the most important attribute of a plant sculpture. A high quality folding job isn't what people see from across the room. Delicate lines and intricate stems don't bring them in for a closer look. What attracts crowds is color, and in this section I'm going to teach you painting methods that don't just garner attention; they keep people's attention and invite them to look more closely.

For the record, my "favorite color" doesn't have a name. It's a color I haven't seen before; one that is a composite of several coats of differently colored paint. It is dynamic, and changes every time I put brush to paper. My favorite color is the one that someone asks, "what do you call that color?"

Over the years I have developed several methods for using color to enhance my origami flowers. Sometimes it's just a matter of shading, or pre-painting an area that's a little bit darker than what will surround it. Other times, I'll take advantage of special relationships some colors have to each other. In general, you can't go wrong. Even if you end up with a color you hadn't envisioned, chances are it will look really neat in a completed sculpture.

My intent here is not just to provide you with a method of painting that will produce good results, but also to provide a window into the dynamic environment that is composite color. Whenever I begin a project I have a color scheme in mind, but my color choices often change during the process of painting. As layers of color get added to the paper they literally compose the overall color; hence the name composite color. I like to make adjustments as I work, and I'm hoping you will too. Perhaps after completing this section your "favorite color" will be like mine.

Painting Leaf Color

I tend to start planning a new sculpture a few days in advance. My first consideration is color. I usually decide on a color scheme which includes some shade of green leaves with contrasting, bright-colored flowers. I always begin by painting the leaf color first. There are several reasons for doing this. The most important is that I won't be able to paint the flowers successfully unless I've already painted a circle of leaf color on the calyx side (green underside) of each piece of flower paper. Another reason is that, because I'm using a composite painting method, my leaves may not come out the exact color I had envisioned. This means I may decide on a different flower color based on the leaf color I obtain.

When I first started making plants from paper, my leaves and flowers often had little white cracks in their surfaces, a by-product that occurs from folding paper. These cracks revealed that my plants weren't real. As my techniques have become more sophisticated, I developed methods for avoiding these cracks. The first step in the process of painting leaf color is to stain the paper, so no one will ever see white paper peeking from beneath a beautiful coat of paint.

Of course a by-product of staining is that the natural grain of the paper becomes more pronounced. This pattern is surprisingly similar to the cellular pattern evident on the leaf surfaces of many plant species. So not only does staining help me downplay the reality that I'm using paper, but it can also add a color complexity that makes my sculptures look more like real plants.

The color I stain with is called the base color. I then add layers of additional colors on top. In this example I begin with green. If I had wanted very dark colored leaves, I might have begun with black. If I wanted light green leaves I would begin with yellow. To maximize the benefit of staining, the final shade should be similar in tone to your base color.

1 Cut paper following the instructions beginning on page 16. In this example I'm preparing paper for a sculpture that will have three leaf sizes, as represented by the three sheets of paper on the left. It will also have Columbine flower assemblies and buds, as represented by the sheets on the right.

2 After cutting you can see that I'm preparing 48 leaves in large, medium and small sizes, as represented by the six rectangles on the left. The four squares on the upper right will become buds. The three large squares below these will be combined with three of the small squares at the bottom to become Columbine flower assemblies (page 92).

3 Create a dilute mixture of acrylic paint and water in a shallow cup. In this example I'm using about 1 part paint to 20 parts water. We're actually staining the paper, not painting it. In other words, this first coat of paint should never be so strong that paint builds up on the surface of the paper.

4 Brush on a thin coat of paint onto what will become your leaf squares. I like to use a chopstick to hold the rectangle in place while I paint it. I use an old magazine to serve as blotting paper under my work.

5 Use your brush to lift a corner of the rectangle and flip it.

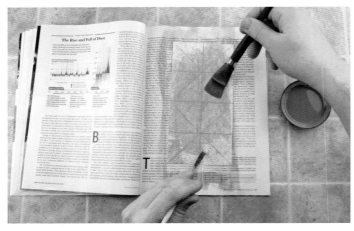

6 Paint the other side. Your rectangle should become completely saturated and semi-translucent.

7 Use your brush to lift a corner and then flip the rectangle onto the opposing page. Brush off excess paint.

8 Use your brush to lift a corner again, and flip it one last time. Use your brush to remove any excess paint from this side. Set the paper aside to dry.

9 Next, paint a circle of leaf color on the calyx side (the side where the diagonals are valley folds) of squares that you're going to use as flowers.

10 Allow the papers to dry ***completely*** before proceeding to the next step.

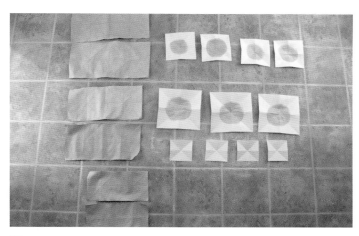

11 It is important to confirm your paper is dry. If you proceed with damp paper it will ***pill***, forming tiny clumps of fibers as your brush runs over it. Your dry paper will feel rough, crispy, and will feel kind of warm.

12 Mix another batch of paint, but this time it should be a bit thicker. It should be 1 part acrylic paint, 1 part artist's medium, and 10 parts water. I'm using dark green and burnt sienna acrylic paint.

13 Paint the top-facing side (you can tell it's top-facing because the diagonal folds will be valley folds) of your leaf sheets with two coats of the mixture. Do the same for the little circles on the calyx side of your flower paper.

14 Mix a different color for your final coat. I like to darken my color a little so I mixed 1 part Van Dyke brown, 1 part artist's medium, and 10 parts water.

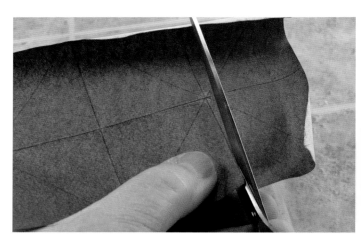

15 When you're happy with your leaf color, cut each rectangle into eight squares and fold them into leaves.

After three coats of a mixture that includes artist's medium, I've got a beautiful finish. It's a complex color, with a visible, natural looking pattern, and a glossy finish that will resist dust.

PAINTING FLOWERS

Painting flowers is similar to painting leaves except that for many varieties you will want to paint a layer of shading before staining your paper. You should have some sort of final color in mind, and then choose a shading color that will react favorably with it. Consider the color table below before you begin.

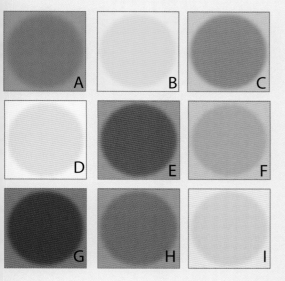

Some color combinations I like: A. Green followed by turquoise. B. Orange followed by yellow. C. Dark blue followed by pink. D. Pink followed by cream. E. Dark blue followed by red. F. Red followed by orange. G. Dark blue followed by purple. H. Black followed by red. I. Orange followed by pink.

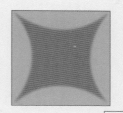

I would like to create a Columbine flower with large orange-red petals and a small cream flower at the center.

So I will begin by painting dark brown shading on my larger flower in the arced pattern, and a circle of dark cream shading for my smaller flower. **Note: Buds do not require shading.**

1 Begin by mixing paint for the shading on the daisy flower; 1 part burnt umber acrylic paint with about ½ part artist's medium and 10 parts water.

2 Paint short lines representing the tips of the arc with a narrow brush.

3 Paint shallow arcs between the lines you painted in step 2.

4 Fill the area inside the arcs with a wide brush.

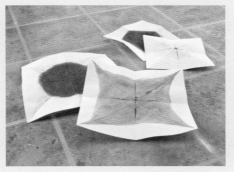

5 Allow the paper to dry completely before proceeding.

6 Next we mix a color similar to what we'd like our finished color to be, and stain with it. I'm mixing 1 part vermilion, 1 part scarlet to about 20 parts water.

7 Stain the flower-top side of your paper and then flip it.

8 And then stain the underside of your paper.

9 I'm planning to fold buds, so I need to stain those with this orange-red color too.

10 Once dry, take an analytical look at the color you have created. What do you like about it and what don't you like? How does it need to be adjusted? In this example, I think the color is a little too red and a little too bright. I'm going to tone it down, and make it more orange.

11 I've got 2 parts vermilion (to increase the orange color), along with 1 part burnt sienna (to tone the color down a bit) and 2 parts artist's medium to which I will add about 10 parts water.

12 Apply two coats of paint to each side of your paper.

13 Now we paint the smaller flowers which will become the center of the Columbine. Mix 1 part burnt umber, ½ part artist's medium, and 10 parts water.

14 Paint a circle of color in the center of your paper with a narrow brush.

15 Fill in the circle with a wide brush.

16 Proceed only when your paper has dried completely.

17 This time I'm going to stain the paper with a light brownish color. I use ½ part burnt sienna, and 2 parts white to 20 parts water.

18 Saturate both sides of your paper just as you did in steps 8 and 9 on the opposite page and allow it to dry completely.

19 Next I combine ½ part vermilion, 2 parts white and 2 parts artist's medium with 10 parts water. I paint two coats of the mixture on the flower side of each piece of paper (the underside will not be seen in the Columbine flower assembly).

20 When you finish painting, inspect your colors. I like what I've got, but I think it would look even better if both my cream and my orange-red sheets got a coat of light yellow. I mix 1 part yellow with 1 part white and 2 parts artist's medium and 10 parts water and apply one coat to each piece of paper.

21 Once you're happy with your colors and your paper has dried, you can fold your flowers and leaves.

Hint: While working I accidentally splattered some red paint on this square. Luckily I only needed three. It's a good idea to make a few extra sheets in case something goes wrong.

The leaves and flowers I made look amazingly real.

Here's a great example of subtle shading. The shadows you see in the center of the Primrose, and in the valleys of the Daisy aren't so much shadows as they are the shading I painted.

How to Obtain a Dark Green

In the early days of exploring this art form, I spent a lot of time trying to obtain a dark green. At first I thought it was a matter of mixing the right proportions of yellow and blue. Then I decided it was a matter painting sufficient layers of paint; this worked but I ended up with a thick coat of paint that self-destructed when it was folded. Finally I realized it was really about overcoming the brilliancy of the white paper. It turns out that staining the paper black solves the problem. It is probably best to stain with green mixed with a little black. A purely black color is hard to overcome, as you'll see in this example.

1 I'm going to make six little flowering plants. In this example I'll use flowers to represent low-to-the-ground foliage as well. So each plant will have one flower and one foliage, or two pieces of paper per plant.

2 I began by painting the shading (the orange tapered lines shown in the photo) on all the flowers (see page 97 steps 3 through 5). Then I stained the foliage pieces with black (see pages 94 and 95, steps 4 through 11), including a little circle of black on the calyx underside of each flower. Finally, I stained each flower yellow.

3 After two coats of dark green (see page 95 steps 12 and 13) I'm still unhappy with the color I've obtained. It's dark, but it doesn't look natural.

4 I painted two more coats of a light, yellowish-green (see page 96, step 14). I now have a richer leaf color. Notice that you can now see the grain, and that the color varies from very dark green to dark green. The paper also has a natural-looking gloss. I'm very happy with this color.

5 After painting two coats of yellow on the flowers (see page 98 steps 11 and 12), I'm ready to fold.

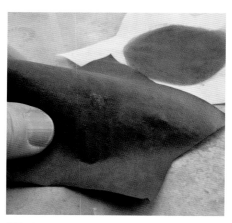

Hint: Obtain dark colored leaves by staining with black.

Notice how the orange shading interacts with the yellow petals. This flower is a Trillium (page 71) and the foliage is a Corolla (page 86).

How to Obtain a Light Green

Just as we used black to create a dark leaf color, we can use yellow to create a light one.

1 Perform steps 4 through 11 on pages 94 and 95, staining your paper with yellow, rather than black.

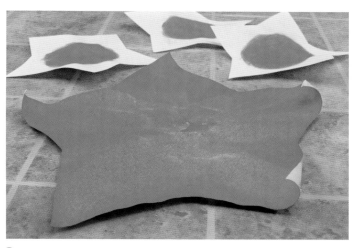

2 Next, paint two coats of green just as you did in steps 12 and 13 on page 95.

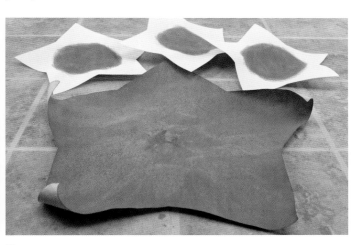

3 Finally, paint one or two more coats just as you did in step 14 on page 96, but using burnt sienna instead of Van Dyke brown.

At first glance I thought this photo was grainy and I needed to change my camera settings. Then I looked at the counter-top in the photo, which isn't grainy. The photo shows the amazingly grainy texture I've achieved in my leaf color.

Hint: When I paint dark blue flowers I use a blackened-blue. Be careful when using black; measure and mix small amounts by squeezing them onto your brush rather than adding them directly.

MAKING ROCKS AND BOULDERS

In the early days of this art form I used real rocks as bases for my sculptures. The rocks served their purpose; they were heavy and kept my sculptures from tipping over. On the few occasions when a sculpture did tip over, or worse yet, was dropped, the rock, with its tremendous amount of kinetic energy, acted much like a wrecking ball on an abandoned building; it smashed, and crashed through the sculpture leaving a path of destruction.

These rocks also made it almost impossible to ship a sculpture. During shipping, the rock would inevitably get loose inside the box, bounce around, and completely destroy the sculpture. On the receiving end, the customer would open their box to discover a rock packed in brightly colored folded paper. "Where's my sculpture?" they would ask.

In 2010 a fellow named Stéphane Verret of Montreal, Canada wrote me and told me that he had made rock-like structures from paper. He said he used a method derived from my makigami technique. I began experimenting, and soon developed the method presented in this section. These rocks made from paper have revolutionized my work. Not only do they make nifty mounts for sculptures, but they also allow me to experiment with textures.

An added benefit of making rocks from paper is that they have very little mass, and thus, very low kinetic energy. Now I am able to ship my sculptures all over the world without fear. And because they're light I save on shipping costs, and I can carry boxes full of them into craft shows with little effort.

If you're going to make rocks and boulders occasionally, perhaps once per month, it will be fine to make them on a countertop as shown in the following pages. This process is unlikely to damage your work surface. However, should you find you need to make rocks and boulders more frequently, I strongly recommend you find a dedicated craft work surface.

Mixing Makigami Solution

The first step to making rocks and boulders is to make some makigami rolling solution. You will need a recycled juice container, a large container of wood glue, and a large container of acrylic paint.

Mix 1 part wood glue, 1 part white acrylic paint, with 20 parts water in a recycled juice container.

How to make Rocks and Boulders

This is an easy method for making rocks and boulders to use as the base for your sculptures.

1 Tear two sheets of newspaper in half so you end up with four half-sheets of newspaper.

2 Put on an apron and latex gloves. Pour makigami solution into a wide bowl. You'll also need a wide brush.

3 Brush a liberal amount of makigami solution onto your work area. The area should be about as big as one of the half-sheets you made in step 1.

4 Fold one of your sheets in half and place it onto your wet work surface, then unfold the remaining portion. This reduces the amount of bubbles under the sheet.

5 Completely saturate the half-sheet with makigami solution.

6 Use your brush to lift a corner and...

7 Carefully flip the half-sheet.

8 Add more makigami solution and inspect to ensure that the half-sheet is completely saturated. Push any air bubbles out to an edge.

9 Carefully lift the right side and then...

10 Using both hands, fold it in half vertically.

11 Use your brush to remove any bubbles and to sharpen the fold.

12 Fold it in half horizontally.

13 Use your brush to remove any bubbles and to sharpen the fold.

14 Fold it in half vertically again.

15 Use your brush to remove any bubbles and sharpen the fold. Set this folded half-sheet aside and repeat steps 1 through 15 on a second half-sheet.

16 Stack the second half-sheet on top of the first. Repeat steps 1 through 11 on a third half-sheet. Hint: To make a larger rock add more sheets.

17 Put your stack of two half-sheets in the center of your third half-sheet. Fold the bottom corners to the center.

18 Fold the upper corners to the center.

19 Fold the bottom edge to the center.

20 Fold the remaining three edges to the center.

21 Your model should look like this. Flip it.

22 Notice that all single-ply paper edges are on the underside. Single-ply edges reveal that we made our rock from paper, so we need to keep them hidden. At the same time we want to keep the bottom of our rock as flat as possible so it will be a stable mount.

23 Put your fingers on top of the outside edges and push toward the center. Allow a shape to develop spontaneously. Squeeze the paper together and against your work surface to ensure the bottom is flat.

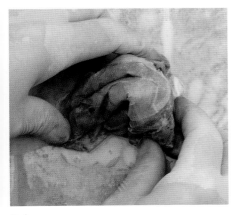

24 Squeeze and pinch to form a rock-like shape.

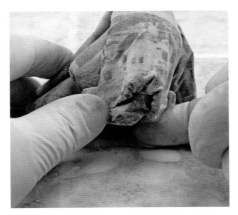

25 Tuck any protruding single-ply edges underneath.

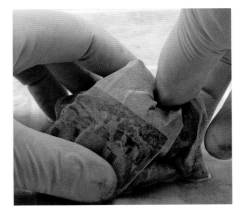

26 Make indentations and crevices where plants can be attached.

27 Put your "rock" in a pan.

28 Put your rock in the sun to cure. It will cure most quickly in a car, parked in the sun, with the windows closed. During winter it can take up to 3 days to cure. In the summer it can take as little as four hours.

29 You can tell when a rock is fully cured by touching it. It should feel warm, and it should weigh about as much as the paper you used to create it. Notice how flat the bottom of the rock is in this picture. A flat bottom is very important for a stable base.

PAINTING THE ROCKS AND BOULDERS

How do you mimic a rock's finish (its color and texture)? There are so many varieties. Some have dull surfaces, others are reflective. My favorite finishes mimic rocks that have been exposed to moving water, like the rocks you'll find in stream beds. They have smooth, highly polished surfaces. The types of rocks and boulders that I make benefit greatly from glossy finishes, and seem not to look quite as good with matte finishes. This is because glossy finishes reflect more light, and therefore are better at hiding mistakes.

I'll never be able to duplicate the finish on this rock because I suspect it is still a work in progress! I am told that this rock must have been at the bottom of a river, picking up and incorporating other, smaller stones over a long period of time.

How to Paint a Faux Bluestone Finish

1 I begin by mixing 1 part phthalo blue, 1/10th part black, 1 part artist's medium and about 5 parts water. This is a messy process, so you'll want to work on top of wax paper and use latex gloves and an apron.

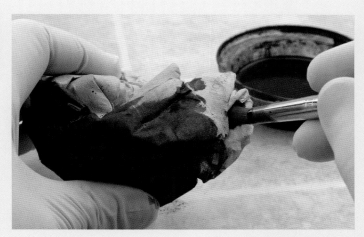

2 Paint the entire surface of your rock. Make an extra effort to ensure that all the nooks and crannies get painted too.

3 Paint about ½ inch (about 1.3 cm) around the edge of the bottom of the rock.

4 Carefully inspect your work to make sure you haven't left any areas unpainted.

5 Allow the finish to dry for at least 4 hours before proceeding. The rock in the foreground is darker because its outer surface had a dark newsprint photo on it. (You can see the original color of these rocks in previous steps.)

6 For the final coat I mix 1 part black, 1 part artist's medium and 5 parts water. I also use a wide brush so I can apply the paint more quickly and liberally.

7 Quickly apply a generous amount of paint to the entire surface of your rock. Don't worry too much about getting the paint into deep crevices, just get the surfaces covered.

8 Rub the rock's surface with your fingers, removing some paint from flat areas, and allowing it to build up in the nooks and crannies.

9 Wipe your fingers on a paper towel frequently to remove excess paint and then continue to rub the surface of your rock.

10 Don't forget to paint the edges of the bottom of the rock.

11 Inspect your rock. You may add a second, or even a third coat if you wish. My rock needed only one coat. You can see the difference in color and finish between the rock that's finished in the foreground and one that hasn't gotten a final coat of paint in the background.

12 I think my completed faux bluestone rocks look beautiful. Now all they need is some plants!

How to Paint a Faux Brown Chert Finish

This is a beautiful, semi-transparent finish that takes advantage of the underlying newspaper colors and print to create a more complex surface.

1 Begin by mixing 1 part burnt umber and 1 part artist's medium with about 5 parts water. Complete steps 2 through 4 on page 107 using this mixture.

2 Your rocks should look like this. Allow them to dry for about four hours.

3 Complete steps 6 through 10 on the opposite page, but this time using Van Dyke Brown rather than black and your rocks should look similar to this.

Print from the outer layer of newspaper is clearly visible in this close-up, but from a distance it simply makes the rock's color look more complex.

INTRODUCTION TO MAKIGAMI

About three years ago I needed a solution. I was attaching flowers and leaves to real branches. Over time these branches dried out and became brittle. Moving the sculptures became a chore of damage mitigation. If I had to move 10 sculptures it was likely I would destroy one and damage at least three more.

Sculptures made from oak branches self-destructed on their own. It began with the shedding of leaves. And then branches would spontaneously abort themselves from the branch. It was tremendously disheartening; to watch, powerlessly, as a sculpture slowly biodegraded. I wondered if perhaps my sculptures could be made from another material.

The obvious material to try was wire. Wire can be easily manipulated and is highly durable. I searched on the Web and found several artists making tree trunks and branch networks from wire. They looked neat, but they also looked the same. One artist's work was hard to distinguish from another's. I also don't like working with wire. It is expensive, cuts your fingers when you twist it, and is far more suitable for doing things like carrying electricity and transmitting data than it is for making branches.

Next I considered paper. I remembered that lollipop sticks are made from paper. I started with white copy paper and tried saturating it with paint and then twisting it. I had marginal success. I then tried to roll it and had more success. I began to run out of copy paper and decided to try that morning's newspaper. It worked unbelievably well. I soon developed a technique for rolling tapered, amazingly real-looking stems.

I needed to give the technique and the material a name. Because origami means folded-paper in Japanese, I felt this new technique ought to have a Japanese name too. My father took particular interest in this process, researching various Japanese words for "roll." He gave me a list of words, but one stood out from the rest. It stood out because I was already familiar with it from eating at Japanese sushi restaurants. The word was *maki* as in California maki, or a California roll; one of my favorite foods. Makigami even sounds nice. So when I refer to *makigami* I am either referring to the technique, the resultant material, or both. As you may have guessed from the title of this section, there is much more information available on makigami. I have written several other books about it. I hope you will enjoy working with this wonderful, recycled and earth-friendly material as much as I do.

Determining Long Fiber Direction

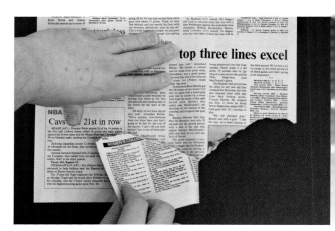

1 Orient a piece of newspaper as shown. Try to tear across the page like I've done. Chances are you'll be unable to easily tear a straight line.

2 Now try tearing up from the bottom. If your newspaper is like mine it will tear easily, and in a relatively straight line. It is easy to tear a straight line when tearing parallel to the longest fibers; difficult when tearing perpendicular to them.

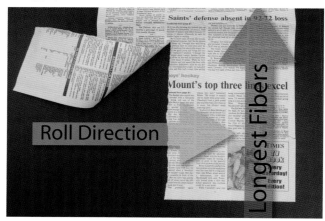

3 We always roll perpendicular to the longest fibers. If the newspaper you're working with doesn't behave like mine did, you will need to adjust all the instructions that follow by rotating your newspaper 90 degrees.

Cutting Newspaper for Origami Ikebana

1 Begin with 3 pages from a newspaper. I'm using one large sheet representing two pages, and a half-sheet which represents one page.

2 Combine the pages as shown and then rotate them so that the fold is furthest from you. Use scissors to cut off the rightmost 8 inches (20 cm) of newspaper.

3 Set aside the larger leftmost piece. Cut all three layers of the rightmost piece as shown, about 5 inches (13 cm) from the bottom.

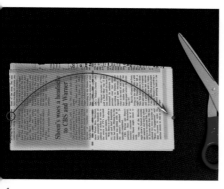

4 You should now have three sheets of paper that are each 8 x 5 inches (20 x 13 cm). Fold all three sheets in half as shown

5 Use your scissors to cut all six layers in the pattern shown by the dashed line and then unfold the fold you made in step 4.

6 We'll be using the bottom three pieces of newspaper. Put the remainder in your recycling bin.

7 You should have three identical pieces of paper.

Rolling Makigami Strips

1 If you haven't already mixed some makigami rolling solution you'll need to do so now. Mix 1 part white acrylic paint, 1 part wood glue, and 20 parts water in a large container.

2 Pour some makigami rolling solution in a wide, heavy, hard-to-tip-over jar. I'm right handed, so I keep my jar of solution to the far right. Next to it are pieces of newspaper I'm going to roll. An old, shallow cookie sheet I use as a rolling tray is directly in front of me; I use a second cookie sheet, on the left, to hold finished strips.

3 Begin by painting a layer of solution onto your rolling pan that is about the size of the piece of paper you're going to roll.

4 Put one piece of newspaper into the solution. Paint on more solution to completely saturate it.

5 Use your brush to lift the newspaper off the pan and then...

6 Flip it.

7 Remove any air bubbles with your brush and confirm that the paper is completely saturated with solution.

8 Fold about ¼ inch (0.6 cm) of the leading edge over.

9 Use your brush to remove any air bubbles and sharpen the fold.

10 Curl the folded edge as shown and begin to roll the paper into a slender tube.

11 Roll the remaining paper onto the tube.

12 Your paper should look like this. Put it back in the pan closest to you.

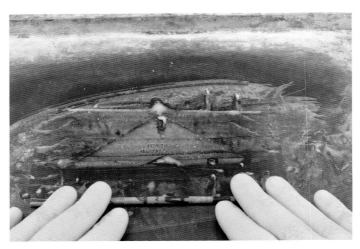

13 Gently roll it away from you.

14 Lift it again and then roll it again.

15 Repeat steps 13 and 14 until you have a solid, tapered shaft of makigami material.

16 Knead the material by pinching and then pushing the makigami into itself as shown. Knead the entire length twice.

17 After kneading your strip should look like this.

18 Roll the strip in the pan a couple more times so it has a smooth, consistent outer layer.

19 Cut the strip in half using a pair of wire cutters.

20 Wrap one of the strips around your right index finger to shape it.

21 Curl the other in the opposite direction by wrapping it around your left index finger to shape it.

22 You should have two little branchlets that curl in opposite directions. Put them in a car parked in the sun and they should cure in about an hour.

Hint: A pair of gloves can be reused up to 20 times. Wash your hands while the gloves are still on. Remove them and allow them to dry. Next time you put them on, put a little talcum powder on your hands to help them fit snugly.

Understanding Taper

It is important that you understand the relationship between the shape of the original piece of paper and the resultant makigami strips. For each piece of paper we make a makigami strip, it will be thickest at its center, and narrowest at both tips. We cut that strip in half so we end up with two pieces of tapered makigami.

The thickest part of our strip is defined by the dimension "C." "B" defines the narrowest. "D" represents the length of the entire strip. If we want a longer strip, we increase the size of "D." If we want a more tapered strip we'd increase the size of "C" and decrease the size of "B."

This method works well for creating short, tapered pieces of makigami. For longer pieces we need to use a slightly different technique.

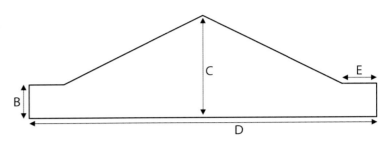

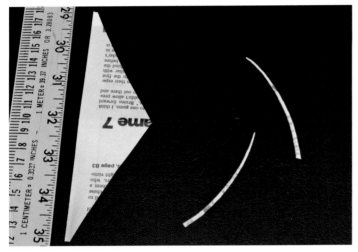

Cut with no "E" and a small "B" and you can make flower stamens and pieces of grass.

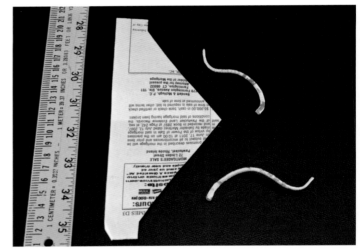

With a cut like this you can make narrow branchlets or shoots for flowers.

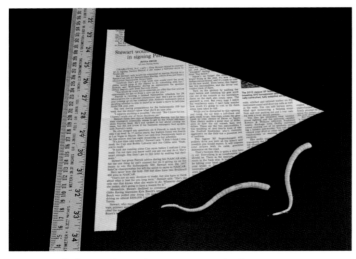

With a large "D" we end up with two nice stems for flowers.

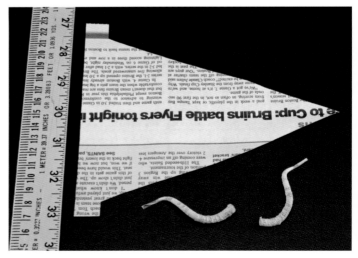

With a small "D" and a large "C" we can make beautiful, highly tapered small branches for a tree.

Making Longer and Thicker Makigami

In the previous section you learned how to make two strips of makigami at a time. That method won't work for making longer strips because of limitations including the size of our rolling pan, and the size of our newspaper. We need to use a different shape to make longer strips of makigami. This alternative shape only makes one strip at a time, but it allows us to add additional layers of paper, so we can make much thicker strips.

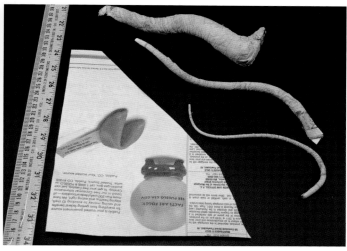

This shape allows us to make longer tapered strips. We can increase the thickness by adding more sheets of identically shaped paper.

If you plan to make thick makigami strips you should also make some narrow curled strips like these. They act as branchlets for leaf connections. These strips are made from rectangles approximately one inch wide by 8 inches long (2.5 x 20 cm). I attach them to a dowel with small pieces of masking tape and allow them to cure.

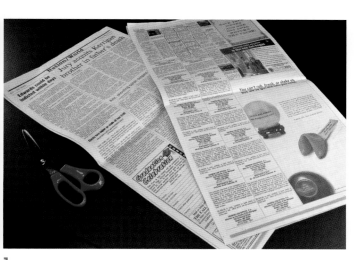

1 Combine several pages of newspaper.

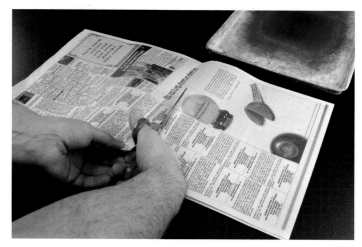

2 Use the narrower side of your rolling pan to measure, and cut off the lower half, just below the fold. ***Remember to always cut towards the long vertical fold.***

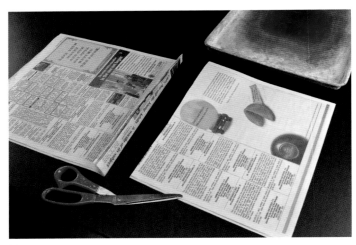

3 Your paper should look like this. Flip the left side and...

4 Insert it into the right side. Align the edge at the bottom.

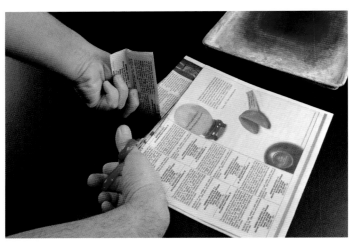

5 Cut the left edge, cutting toward the newspaper's vertical fold, so that all the edges will be even.

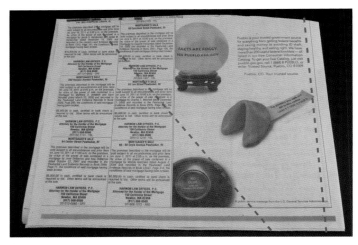

6 With the folded edge on the right, cut the newspaper as shown.

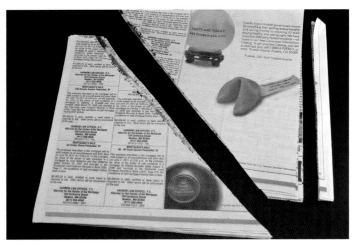

7 Your newspaper should look like this. Recycle the narrow pieces on the right and combine the other two stacks of paper.

8 Make sure the pieces fit in your pan; if they don't trim the tips of the pointy end as shown.

9 Follow steps 3 through 18 beginning on page 112 to roll one strip. Prepare a second strip to be rolled, but after folding the lead edge (see steps 8 and 9 on page 113), place the first strip on top as shown.

10 Curl the new layer of paper around the strip and then roll it. Roll it several times, then *gently* knead it once. You can add as many layers as you wish to increase the thickness of your strip.

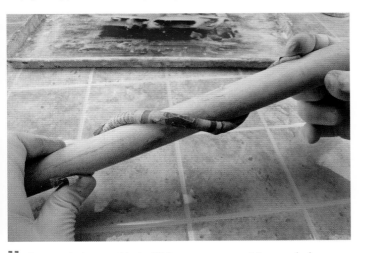

11 Once you're happy with the thickness, wrap your strip around a broom handle or dowel to give it an initial shape, then shape the strip as you see fit. Be careful not to make your strip curve too tightly. The thicker the strip, the less it will bend without tearing.

12 Your makigami may delaminate if you work on shaping it for too long. If it delaminates, put it back in the pan and roll it again.

13 Put your makigami in a car parked in the sun to cure. Narrow strips will cure in a few hours; very thick strips could take a day or two, depending on the season. Your makigami is cured when it is light, dry, and slightly warm to the touch.

Makigami Finishes

In this book I present two basic finishes. I like to begin with a light color and end with a darker one. This emphasizes complexities in the surface of the makigami strip. You can experiment and develop your own finishes.

Two finishes are presented in this book. The green finish is for faster-growing plants like annual flowers, the brown is for slow-growing plants like trees.

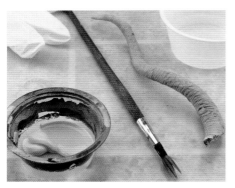

1 To reduce cleanup time, work on top of wax paper and wear one latex glove. Begin by mixing 1 part yellow acrylic paint, 1 part wood glue and 3 parts water.

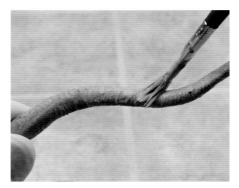

2 Paint a thick coat of the mixture onto your makigami and then allow it to dry for a couple hours.

3 For the brighter green finish shown here, mix 1 part green acrylic paint, 1 part wood glue and 5 parts water. If you desire the darker brown finish, substitute burnt umber acrylic paint for the green.

4 Paint your makigami strip with the mixture. Because this mixture is thinner, you should be able to see through it to the yellow below.

5 Allow your makigami to dry for a couple of hours and it should look like this.

6 If you use burnt umber acrylic paint in step 3, rather than green, your makigami will look like this.

ASSEMBLING ORIGAMI IKEBANA

First, just to be clear, let's call this ikebana-*inspired* origami, because a quick search of book titles reveals that there are over 600 books about ikebana in the English language. If I could perform the same search in Japanese, we would probably discover thousands more. Ikebana is an esoteric subject, with a few specialists, and many professing knowledge. I make no such claim. In writing a book where only one section is dedicated to the subject of ikebana, it would be a challenge beyond my ability to include more than a modicum of the spirit of this art.

From the very start however, ikebana translates poorly into English. The common definition is Japanese flower arranging, which is not quite accurate. A more accurate translation, based on the characters making up the Japanese word (生け花), reveals a different meaning. The first two symbols, 生け, mean keep alive. The third symbol, 花, means flowers. In English keep alive flowers would mean to preserve them, and that would completely miss the spirit of this art form. More loosely translated, the three characters also mean living flowers in English. My research suggests that the meaning behind the concept, living flowers, conveys a more accurate portrayal of what people are trying to achieve when making an ikebana-style flower arrangement. My understanding is that ikebana is about our relationship to the natural world around us. It is an attempt to build balance, or a bridge, between what surrounds us; man-made things like walls, furniture, and decorations, and the living flowers in our arrangement. This is no simple task. I'd like to show you pictures of spaces and then show how an arrangement can interact with that space, but this would require many more pages than can fit in this book. So, I urge you to obtain additional reading material on this art form so that your creations will more accurately reflect the spirit of ikebana. (Check out *Ikebana: The Art of Arranging Flowers* by Shozo Sato, Tuttle Publishing, 2013.)

Based on what I've seen, good-looking ikebana arrangements have several common attributes. If we turn those common attributes into a set of rules for origami ikebana, perhaps we'll have a starting point for making some truly beautiful sculptures. Here are the rules I would suggest you try to follow when making origami ikebana arrangements:

INCORPORATE A SCALENE TRIANGLE
A scalene triangle is a triangle where no sides are equal in length. Perhaps the shape of the foliage forms the scalene, or three flowers define the points of the scalene. The scalene could reflect components of the space where it is going to be installed. Perhaps the shelf upon which the sculpture rests, and the wall it is adjacent to are reflected in two sides of the scalene triangle?

VASTLY VARYING HEIGHT
Try to include plant varieties that vary greatly in terms of their heights. Short flowers and tall grass make for a nice contrast in height, but also consider the space where the sculpture will be on display. How can you use the height of your plants to make the space more attractive?

VASTLY VARYING SHAPE
Contrasting shapes, such as Rotundifolius Leaves in contrast with straight blades of grass, fulfill the spirit of this rule. It is important to reflect the shape, in some form, of the space where the sculpture will be displayed. For example, if I were making a sculpture that were on display below an arched opening, I would try to include a geometric feature either similar to the arch, or in direct contrast to it.

ONE PERSPECTIVE
Design your sculpture to be viewed from one specific perspective. Maximize the visual complexity that is seen from one angle. When designing for a specific space, at what angle will the sculpture be seen? At what height will the viewer be looking? If the sculpture looks great from any angle, that's an added bonus, but try to design it so that one, specific view is best.

COLOR
Color is the single most important attribute of your work. When planning your sculpture, try to find colors that will compliment the surroundings. Using a color from trim or wallpaper nearby is not a bad idea. Using white when the only color surrounding your sculpture is white is probably a mistake, although I've seen amazing things done with shades of gray.

A Simple Assembly

Your first assembly should be kept as simple as possible. In this example I'm going to assemble an origami ikebana from three small flowering plants and some short grass.

1 Gather the components of your sculpture and plan out the colors. I have very dark, short foliage so I've chosen a lighter stone color to contrast with it. The lighter, yellowish-orange color also coordinates with my flowers.

2 Determine how your plants will interact with the rock. I'll be inserting my plants into crevices in the rock. Notice how the foliage stands out against the color of the rock.

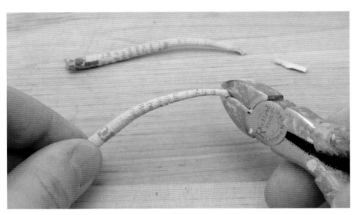

3 Trim your makigami stems, removing any paper that delaminated. (This photo shows unpainted stems being trimmed, but yours should be painted at this stage.)

4 Next, assemble the flowers. Begin by poking a hole in the tip of the bud of each of the flowers.

5 Put a small amount of hot melt glue onto the wide end of one of your stems and then insert it into center of the green flower you're using to represent the foliage.

6 Put a small amount of hot melt glue on the narrow end of your stem and attach the flower to it.

7 Mount each plant onto your rock with hot melt glue. It is best to insert the base of each plant into a crevice or nook.

8 I like to cut my grass so that each is a different height. Then I dip each piece into glue and insert them into a crevice.

9 Mix a solution of 1 part acrylic paint, 1 part wood glue and 3 parts water into a color that matches the stems of your plants. Paint this mixture onto the hot melt glue you used to attach the flower to the stem.

10 If you want to add stamens to your flowers, use the same method used to attach grass (step 8, above). I don't have a lot of space in the center of my flowers so I added only three stamens to each flower. Normally I would have added five.

11 Now look at your sculpture. What do you like about it, and what do you dislike? Look at the rules on page 121. Are there any rules my sculpture breaks? In my opinion, my sculpture doesn't have enough variation in height. I think I'll attach a tall piece of makigami grass using hot melt glue.

12 think my completed sculpture is quite beautiful. It has bright yellow, green, and scarlet colors with a brownish orange rock base. It also has a tall piece of gently curving grass. Several scalene triangles can be drawn; between the flowers, between the foliage, and between the tip of the top of the grass and any two flowers. The shapes of the flowers are similar; however they're vastly different from the grasses which are also different from each other. My sculpture is best viewed from the perspective in this photograph, but it is quite beautiful from any angle.

A More Complex Assembly

In this example we'll build an assembly of makigami strips to form a stem with multiple flowers in the center of our primary plant. We will also consider the space surrounding our sculpture in its construction. This interaction between the space where the sculpture is displayed and the sculpture itself is one of the keys to creating successful ikebana-inspired work.

1 Consider your space. I have a round topped table with a white tablecloth surrounded by a bamboo room divider. This scene has only a few discernable features; a white tablecloth, and long vertical lines created by the bamboo screen. I will use vertical lines, and white, to bridge the gap between this space and nature through an ikebana-style arrangement.

2 I will create a sculpture with very tall, straight grass (the long, straight makigami strips), and a flowering shrub with three dark blue flowers on a gently curving main stem with two shoots, all of which will be mounted on a rock with a dark, Van Dyke brown finish. The flowers are five petal Hippeastrum (page 72), and the foliage is a five petal Corolla (page 86).

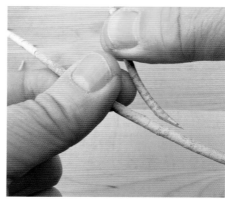

3 Two of my flowers will be attached to shoots which must be attached to the main stem. I cut the makigami shoots at an angle so they will have a natural-looking connection.

I think my completed sculpture looks fantastic. Notice the tall grass. The longest blade is perfectly vertical. It is followed by two shorter pieces that have been attached at angles. Together, all three tips form a curve. Also notice the gently curved bright white stamens, and how they match the bright white tablecloth. It's as if the plant sucked up the color from the tablecloth and inserted it into the stamens. I think this arrangement represents an interesting bridge between nature and its man-made surroundings.

4 I use hot melt glue to attach the shoot to the main stem. I use the hot tip of my glue gun to make the edges of the glued connection smooth.

Hint: Put a damp paper towel into a shallow cup. Dip your index finger and thumb into the cup and then pinch a flower petal. Wait a moment for the moisture to be absorbed by the petal. Then add a graceful curve to the petal. When it dries, the petal will remain curved forever.

Complex Assemblies

In order to mimic the greatest possible variety of plants, I will describe how to create more complex assemblies. Volumes could be written on this subject. You will find far more detailed information in my book *Advanced Origami Bonsai* (Coleman, 2009). The following pages are here as a primer, to whet your appetite, and to motivate you to try this sometimes complex, but truly rewarding art form. The example which follows will be wall-mounted rather than free-standing.

1 I will be making a fairly complex Columbine plant sculpture (page 192). I have made several makigami stems, branches, and one curly piece of makigami to act as branchlets.

2 First, I temporarily attach my longest stems to my rock using hot melt glue.

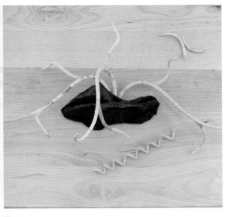

3 Next I use hot melt glue to attach some short branches I've made. These branches will provide a place to attach leaves. Branches ending with their tips pointing directly away from my work surface will have flowers attached to them.

4 The last step of building the stem structure is to cut, and attach, with hot melt glue, little branchlets cut from the curly piece of makigami. I cut one end of the branchlet at a shallow angle, and the other end straight.

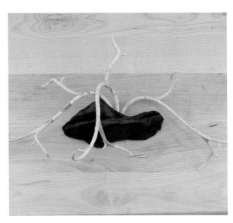

5 Here is my completed assembly. Now I carefully remove the stems from the rock for finishing. I'll use the tip of my hot melt glue gun to liquefy the glue, but it's almost impossible to remove the stems without causing a little bit of damage to the rock.

6 As you can see, I've torn a small amount of paper on my rock, which I'll be able to touch up later. Most importantly, now I can make the connections between branches, stems and branchlets smooth as I did in step 4 on the opposite page. Then I can paint the assemblies as I demonstrated on page 120.

7 Now I reattach my stems, but in a more substantial way, using more hot melt glue than I used the first time. I also prepare to attach leaves and flowers, and consider the viewing perspective of my sculpture as it relates to the leaves.

8 I have decided to attach leaves in pairs to each branchlet. Each pair of leaves will be attached so that their surfaces are parallel to my work surface.

9 Perspective is important—this piece is designed to be viewed from the front. When viewed from the side, you can only see the edges of my leaves.

10 When viewed from the front, the proper perspective, you can clearly see all of my leaves.

11 This is a wall hanging sculpture so I'll need to attach a hanger. The first step is to consider the center of gravity of the sculpture. I need to make sure there's more weight below the hanger than above it. This ensures that the sculpture will hang properly on my wall.

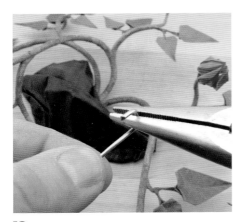

12 I begin by bending a right angled U-shape (the hanger) into a piece of wire. Next I bend a tighter curved U-shape, and use my pliers to secure the wire around my stem.

13 Once the wire is secure, I paint it the same color as the stem to which it's attached.

14 I also touch-up the connection I re-glued in step 7 with a color similar to my rock.

15 I added a few blades of grass to complete the sculpture.

Tip: Sometimes it's a good idea to prototype plants before actually making them. I invested over 100 hours in creating the fern plant pictured here. I want the flowering plant to interact with, not overpower, the fern plant. By prototyping the flowering plant I can see how the plants will interact without investing a lot of time. This prototype lead me to change the shape of the flowering plant's stem.

Three five-petal Hippeastrum flowers bloom from a single stem while three pieces of long grass grow in the background.

Three red Lady Slippers cling to the side of a rock.

A Morning Glory plant grows around a brown dowel.

Notice how the long white stamens compliment the dark blue flowers.

Even traditional, four-petal flowers benefit from stamens.

Assembling Lady Slipper plants.

Blue Lady Slippers hover over a lush fern plant. The fern is made up of 180 leaflets in 8 sizes.

Three small flowers cling to this vertically mounted sculpture. The fern is made up of leaflets that were made in 20 sizes.